EXPLORATIONS IN THE FUNCTIONS OF LANGUAGE

M.A.K. Halliday

ELSEVIER

NEW YORK OXFORD AMSTERDAM

ELSEVIER NORTH-HOLLAND, INC.
52 Vanderbilt Avenue, New York, NY 10017

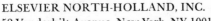

First published 1973, reprinted 1974
by Edward Arnold (Publishers) Ltd.

Elsevier North-Holland edition
published in 1977

Calligraphy in cover design adapted from
Calligraphy by Arthur Baker. © 1973 by Arthur Baker.
Published by Dover Publications, Inc.

Library of Congress Cataloging in Publication Data
Halliday, Michael Alexander Kirkwood.
    Explorations in the functions of language.

    Includes bibliographical references.
    1. Language and languages—Addresses, essays,
lectures. 2. Linguistics—Addresses, essays, lectures.
I. Title.
P49.H34 1977   410   76-57229
ISBN 0-444-00201-4

Printed in the United States of America

Contents

Publisher's Introduction

This book, *Explorations in the Functions of Language* by M.A.K. Halliday, is part of a series entitled *Explorations in Language Study* published in Great Britain by Edward Arnold Limited under the general editorship of Peter Doughty and Geoffrey Thornton. We are publishing selected books from this series because of the importance and relevance of the material to American educators. Other volumes available for sale from Elsevier include *Learning How to Mean,* also by M.A.K. Halliday, and *Language Study: The School and the Community,* which comprises three previously published essays in the series by Peter Doughty, Geoffrey Thornton, and Anne Doughty. Additional volumes in *Explorations in Language Study* will be forthcoming.

Foreword

In the course of our efforts to develop a linguistic focus for work in English language, now published as *Language in Use*, we came to realize the extent of the growing interest in what we would call a linguistic approach to language. Lecturers in Colleges and Departments of Education see the relevance of such an approach in the education of teachers. Many teachers in schools and in colleges of Further Education see themselves that 'Educational failure is primarily *linguistic* failure', and have turned to Linguistic Science for some kind of exploration and practical guidance. Many of those now explorind the problems of relationships, community or society, from a sociological or psychological point of view wish to make use of a linguistic approach to the language in so far as it is relevant to these problems.

We were conscious of the wide divergence between the aims of the linguist, primarily interested in language as a system for organizing 'meanings', and the needs of those who now wanted to gain access to the insights that resulted from that interest. In particular, we were aware of the wide gap that separated the literature of academic Linguistics from the majority of those who wished to find out what Linguistic Science might have to say about language and the use of language.

Out of this experience emerged our own view of that much used term, 'Language Study', developed initially in the chapters of *Exploring Language*, and now given expression in this series. Language Study is not a subject, but a process, which is why the series is to be called *Explorations in Language Study*. Each exploration is focused upon a meeting point between the insights of Linguistic Science, often in conjunction with other social sciences, and the linguistic questions raised by the study of a particular aspect of individual behaviour or human society.

Initially, the volumes in the series have a particular relevance to the role of language in teaching and learning. The editors intend that they should make a basic contribution to the literature of Language Study, doing justice equally to the findings of the academic disciplines involved and the practical needs of those who now want to take a linguistic view of their own particular problems of language and the use of language.

Peter Doughty
Geoffrey Thornton

Introduction

The five papers that make up this book are linked by a common theme. They are all concerned with exploring a functional approach to the study of language.

A functional approach to language means, first of all, investigating how language is used: trying to find out what are the purposes that language serves for us, and how we are able to achieve these purposes through speaking and listening, reading and writing. But it also means more than this. It means seeking to explain the nature of language in functional terms: seeing whether language itself has been shaped by use, and if so, in what ways— how the form of language has been determined by the functions it has evolved to serve.

The first paper, 'Relevant models of language', suggests a functional interpretation of the child's early language development. When a child begins to learn his mother tongue, he is, in effect, learning new modes and conditions of being, and his progress consists in mastering one by one a small set of basic functions of language, such as the instrumental or 'I want' function, the regulatory or 'do as I tell you' function, and so on. In other words, he is learning how to mean; and the meaning potential that he is building up is a measure of what he can do with language.

In the second paper, 'The functional basis of language', we attempt to relate these developmental functions, those which the child comes to master in the course of learning his mother tongue, to a functional theory of the adult language. For the adult language the notion of function has to be sharpened and refined; it is no longer equivalent to a generalized notion of 'use', but is a more abstract concept relating to the grammatical principle on which all human language is organized. Moreover, whereas the young child at first tends to use language in just one function at a time, with the adult almost every instance of language involves all functions at once, in subtle and complex interactions. In order to understand how the adult language system develops out of its early origins, we have to find the common thread that runs through the concept of 'functions of language', uniting both its humbler and its more sophisticated senses.

Paper 3, 'Language in a social perspective', suggests an interpretation of the functioning of language in socially significant contexts. This is illustrated by reference to Professor Bernstein's theories of social order and social change, theories in which language plays an essential part. Language is the primary means for the transmission of culture from one generation to the next; and Bernstein's work has shown that there are certain types of social context, especially forms of interaction between parent and child, which are critical for this socialization process. By taking a functional viewpoint we can gain some idea of how it is that ordinary language, in its everyday uses, can so effectively transmit to the child the deepest patterns of the culture; and in the fourth paper, 'Towards a sociological semantics', we attempt to formulate some general principles for this kind of 'socio-semantics', in which meaning is related both to the internal structure of language and to the social contexts in which language operates. Meanings are expressed through grammatical patterns; but meanings are themselves the expression, or realization, of options in behaviour, and some of these options have a broad socio-cultural significance.

In the final paper, 'Linguistic function and literary style', the same general notions are taken up and applied to the study of literature, the text being William Golding's novel *The Inheritors*. The suggestion is that the key to the study of style lies in semantics, and that an approach to style through semantics implies a functional interpretation of meaning. This enables us to relate meaning in language to the wider background of semiotics as a whole.

The notion 'functions of language' is perhaps not as straightforward as it appears at first sight. We cannot simply equate 'function' with 'use'; instead we must be prepared to take a more general and, in the context of the adult language system, a more abstract view of the nature of linguistic function. But at the same time, just because it is so general, and theoretical, in its implications, the concept of linguistic function is an important one for the understanding of language in its educational, developmental, social and aesthetic aspects.

M. A. K. Halliday

1 Relevant models of language

The teacher of English who, when seeking an adequate definition of language to guide him in his work, meets with a cautious 'well, it depends on how you look at it' is likely to share the natural impatience felt by anyone who finds himself unable to elicit 'a straight answer to a straight question'. But the very frequency of this complaint may suggest that, perhaps, questions are seldom as straight as they seem. The question 'what is language?', in whatever guise it appears, is as diffuse and, at times, disingenuous as other formulations of its kind, for example 'what is literature?' Such questions, which are wisely excluded from examinations, demand the privilege of a qualified and perhaps circuitous answer.

In a sense the only satisfactory response is 'why do you want to know?', since unless we know what lies beneath the question we cannot hope to answer it in a way which will suit the questioner. Is he interested in language planning in multilingual communities? Or in aphasia and language disorders? Or in words and their histories? Or in dialects and those who speak them? Or in how one language differs from another? Or in the formal properties of language as a system? Or in the functions of language and the demands that we make on it? Or in language as an art medium? Or in the information and redundancy of writing systems? Each one of these and other such questions is a possible context for a definition of language. In each case language 'is' something different.

The criterion is one of relevance; we want to understand, and to highlight, those facets of language which bear on the investigation or the task in hand. In an educational context the problem for linguistics is to elaborate some account of language that is relevant to the work of the English teacher. What constitutes a relevant notion of language from his point of view, and by what criteria

1

can this be decided? Much of what has recently been objected to, among the attitudes and approaches to language that are current in the profession, arouses criticism not so much because it is false as because it is irrelevant. When, for example, the authors of *The Linguistic Sciences and Language Teaching* suggested that teaching the do's and don'ts of grammar to a child who is linguistically unsuccessful is like teaching a starving man how to hold a knife and fork, they were not denying that there is a ritual element in our use of language, with rules of conduct to which everyone is expected to conform; they were simply asserting that the view of language as primarily good manners was of little relevance to educational needs. Probably very few people ever held this view explicitly; but it was implicit in a substantial body of teaching practices, and if it has now largely been discarded this is because its irrelevance became obvious in the course of some rather unhappy experience.

It is not necessary, however, to sacrifice a generation of children, or even one classroomful, in order to demonstrate that particular preconceptions of language are inadequate or irrelevant. In place of a negative and somewhat hit-and-miss approach, a more fruitful procedure is to seek to establish certain general, positive criteria of relevance. These will relate, ultimately, to the demands that we make of language in the course of our lives. We need therefore to have some idea of the nature of these demands; and we shall try to consider them here from the point of view of the child. We shall ask, in effect, about the child's image of language: what is the 'model' of language that he internalizes as a result of his own experience? This will help us to decide what is relevant to the teacher, since the teacher's own view of language must at the very least encompass all that the child knows language to be.

The child knows what language is because he knows what language does. The determining elements in the young child's experience are the successful demands on language that he himself has made, the particular needs that have been satisfied by language for him. He has used language in many ways—for the satisfaction of material and intellectual needs, for the mediation of personal relationships, the expression of feelings and so on. Language in all these uses has come within his own direct experience, and because of this he is subconsciously aware that language has many functions that affect him personally. Language is, for the child, a rich and adaptable instrument for the realization of his intentions; there is hardly any limit to what he can do with it.

2

As a result, the child's internal 'model' of language is a highly complex one; and most adult notions of language fail to match up to it. The adult's ideas about language may be externalized and consciously formulated, but they are nearly always much too simple. In fact it may be more helpful, in this connection, to speak of the child's 'models' of language, in the plural, in order to emphasize the many-sidedness of his linguistic experience. We shall try to identify the models of language with which the normal child is endowed by the time he comes to school at the age of five; the assumption being that if the teacher's own 'received' conception of language is in some ways less rich or less diversified it will be irrelevant to the educational task.

We tend to underestimate both the total extent and the functional diversity of the part played by language in the life of the child. His interaction with others, which begins at birth, is gradually given form by language, through the process whereby at a very early age language already begins to mediate in every aspect of his experience. It is not only as the child comes to act on and to learn about his environment that language comes in; it is there from the start in his achievement of intimacy and in the expression of his individuality. The rhythmic recitation of nursery rhymes and jingles is still language, as we can see from the fact that children's spells and chants differ from one language to another: English nonsense is quite distinct from French nonsense, because the one is English and the other French. All these contribute to the child's total picture of language 'at work'.

Through such experiences, the child builds up a very positive impression—one that cannot be verbalized, but is none the less real for that—of what language is and what it is for. Much of his difficulty with language in school arises because he is required to accept a stereotype of language that is contrary to the insights he has gained from his own experience. The traditional first 'reading and writing' tasks are a case in point, since they fail to coincide with his own convictions about the nature and uses of language.

*   *   *

Perhaps the simplest of the child's models of language, and one of the first to be evolved, is what we may call the INSTRUMENTAL model. The child becomes aware that language is used as a means of getting things done. About a generation ago, zoologists were finding out about the highly developed mental powers of chimpanzees; and one of the observations described was of the animal

3

that constructed a long stick out of three short ones and used it to dislodge a bunch of bananas from the roof of its cage. The human child, faced with the same problem, constructs a sentence. He says 'I want a banana'; and the effect is the more impressive because it does not depend on the immediate presence of the bananas. Language is brought in to serve the function of 'I want', the satisfaction of material needs. Success in this use of language does not in any way depend on the production of well-formed adult sentences; a carefully contextualized yell may have substantially the same effect, and although this may not be language there is no very clear dividing line between, say, a noise made on a commanding tone and a full-dress imperative clause.

The old *See Spot run. Run, Spot, run!* type of first reader bore no relation whatsoever to this instrumental function of language. This by itself does not condemn it, since language has many other functions besides that of manipulating and controlling the environment. But it bore little apparent relation to any use of language, at least to any with which the young child is familiar. It is not recognizable as language in terms of the child's own intentions, of the meanings that he has reason to express and to understand. Children have a very broad concept of the meaningfulness of language, in addition to their immense tolerance of inexplicable tasks; but they are not accustomed to being faced with language which, in their own functional terms, has no meaning at all, and the old-style reader was not seen by them as language. It made no connection with language in use.

Language as an instrument of control has another side to it, since the child is well aware that language is also a means whereby others exercise control over him. Closely related to the instrumental model, therefore, is the REGULATORY model of language. This refers to the use of language to regulate the behaviour of others. Bernstein and his colleagues have studied different types of regulatory behaviour by parents in relation to the process of socialization of the child, and their work provides important clues concerning what the child may be expected to derive from this experience in constructing his own model of language. To adapt one of Bernstein's examples, as described by Turner, the mother who finds that her small child has carried out of the supermarket, unnoticed by herself or by the cashier, some object that was not paid for, may exploit the power of language in various ways, each of which will leave a slightly different trace or after-image of this role of language in the mind of the child. For example, she may

4

say *you mustn't take things that don't belong to you* (control through conditional prohibition based on a categorization of objects in terms of a particular social institution, that of ownership); *that was very naughty* (control through categorization of behaviour in terms of opposition approved/disapproved); *if you do that again I'll smack you* (control through threat of reprisal linked to repetition of behaviour); *you'll make Mummy very unhappy if you do that* (control through emotional blackmail); *that's not allowed* (control through categorization of behaviour as governed by rule) and so on. A single incident of this type by itself has little significance; but such general types of regulatory behaviour, through repetition and reinforcement, determine the child's specific awareness of language as a means of behavioural control.

The child applies this awareness, in his own attempts to control his peers and siblings; and this in turn provides the basis for an essential component in his range of linguistic skills, the language of rules and instructions. Whereas at first he can make only simple unstructured demands, he learns as time goes on to give ordered sequences of instructions, and then progresses to the further stage where he can convert sets of instructions into rules, including conditional rules, as in explaining the principles of a game. Thus his regulatory model of language continues to be elaborated, and his experience of the potentialities of language in this use further increases the value of the model.

Closely related to the regulatory function of language is its function in social interaction, and the third of the models that we may postulate as forming part of the child's image of language is the INTERACTIONAL model. This refers to the use of language in the interaction between the self and others. Even the closest of the child's personal relationships, that with his mother, is partly and, in time, largely mediated through language; his interaction with other people, adults and children, is very obviously maintained linguistically. (Those who come nearest to achieving a personal relationship that is not linguistically mediated, apparently, are twins.)

Aside, however, from his experience of language in the maintenance of permanent relationships, the neighbourhood and the activities of the peer group provide the context for complex and rapidly changing interactional patterns which make extensive and subtle demands on the individual's linguistic resources. Language is used to define and consolidate the group, to include and to exclude, showing who is 'one of us' and who is not; to impose status, and to contest status that is imposed; and humour, ridicule, deception, persuasion, all the forensic and theatrical arts of language are brought into play. Moreover, the young child, still primarily a learner, can do what very few adults can do in such situations: he can be internalizing language while listening and talking. He can be, effectively, both a participant and an observer at the same time, so that his own critical involvement in this complex interaction does not prevent him from profiting linguistically from it.

Again there is a natural link here with another use of language, from which the child derives what we may call the PERSONAL model. This refers to his awareness of language as a form of his own individuality. In the process whereby the child becomes aware of himself, and in particular in the higher stages of that process, the development of his personality, language plays an essential role. We are not talking here merely of 'expressive' language—language used for the direct expression of feelings and attitudes—but also of the personal element in the interactional function of language, since the shaping of the self through interaction with others is very much a language-mediated process. The child is enabled to offer to someone else that which is unique to himself, to make public his own individuality; and this in turn reinforces and creates this individuality. With the normal child, his awareness of himself is closely bound up with speech: both with hearing himself speak, and with having at his disposal the range of behavioural options that constitute language. Within the concept of the self as an actor, having discretion, or freedom of choice, the 'self as a speaker' is an important component.

Thus for the child language is very much a part of himself, and the 'personal' model is his intuitive awareness of this, and of the way in which his individuality is identified and realized through language. The other side of the coin, in this process, is the child's growing understanding of his environment, since the environment is, first of all, the 'non-self', that which is separated out in the course of establishing where he himself begins and ends. So, fifthly, the child has a HEURISTIC model of language, derived from his knowledge of how language has enabled him to explore his environment.

The heuristic model refers to language as a means of investigating reality, a way of learning about things. This scarcely needs comment, since every child makes it quite obvious that this is what language is for by his habit of constantly asking questions.

When he is questioning, he is seeking not merely facts but explanations of facts, the generalizations about reality that language makes it possible to explore. Again, Bernstein has shown the importance of the question-and-answer routine in the total setting of parent–child communication and the significance of the latter, in turn, in relation to the child's success in formal education: his research has demonstrated a significant correlation between the mother's linguistic attention to the child and the teacher's assessment of the child's success in the first year of school.

The young child is very well aware of how to use language to learn, and may be quite conscious of this aspect of language before he reaches school; many children already control a metalanguage for the heuristic function of language, in that they know what a 'question' is, what an 'answer' is, what 'knowing' and 'understanding' mean, and they can talk about these things without difficulty. Mackay and Thompson have shown the importance of helping the child who is learning to read and write to build up a language for talking about language; and it is the heuristic function which provides one of the foundations for this, since the child can readily conceptualize and verbalize the basic categories of the heuristic model. To put this more concretely, the normal five-year-old either already uses words such as *question, answer* in their correct meanings or, if he does not, is capable of learning to do so.

The other foundation for the child's 'language about language' is to be found in the imaginative function. This also relates the child to his environment, but in a rather different way. Here, the child is using language to create his own environment; not to learn about how things are but to make them as he feels inclined. From his ability to create, through language, a world of his own making he derives the IMAGINATIVE model of language; and this provides some further elements of the metalanguage, with words like *story*, *make up* and *pretend*.

Language in its imaginative function is not necessarily 'about' anything at all: the child's linguistically created environment does not have to be a make-believe copy of the world of experience, occupied by people and things and events. It may be a world of pure sound, made up of rhythmic sequences of rhyming or chiming syllables; or an edifice of words in which semantics has no part, like a house built of playing cards in which face values are irrelevant. Poems, rhymes, riddles and much of the child's own linguistic play reinforce this model of language, and here too the

7

meaning of what is said is not primarily a matter of content. In stories and dramatic games, the imaginative function is, to a large extent, based on content; but the ability to express such content is still, for the child, only one of the interesting facets of language, one which for many purposes is no more than an optional extra.

So we come finally to the REPRESENTATIONAL model. Language is, in addition to all its other guises, a means of communicating about something, of expressing propositions. The child is aware that he can convey a message in language, a message which has specific reference to the processes, persons, objects, abstractions, qualities, states and relations of the real world around him.

This is the only model of language that many adults have; and a very inadequate model it is, from the point of view of the child. There is no need to go so far as to suggest that the transmission of content is, for the child, the least important function of language; we have no way of evaluating the various functions relatively to one another. It is certainly not, however, one of the earliest to come into prominence; and it does not become a dominant function until a much later stage in the development towards maturity. Perhaps it never becomes in any real sense the dominant function; but it does, in later years, tend to become the dominant *model*. It is very easy for the adult, when he attempts to formulate his ideas about the nature of language, to be simply unaware of most of what language means to the child; this is not because he no longer uses language in the same variety of different functions (one or two may have atrophied, but not all), but because only one of these functions, in general, is the subject of conscious attention, so that the corresponding model is the only one to be externalized. But this presents what is, for the child, a quite unrealistic picture of language, since it accounts for only a small fragment of his total awareness of what language is about.

The representational model at least does not conflict with the child's experience. It relates to one significant part of it; rather a small part, at first, but nevertheless real. In this it contrasts sharply with another view of language which we have not mentioned because it plays no part in the child's experience at all, but which might be called the 'ritual' model of language. This is the image of language internalized by those for whom language is a means of showing how well one was brought up; it downgrades language to the level of table-manners. The ritual element in the use of language is probably derived from the interactional, since language in its ritual function also serves to define and delimit a social group; but it has none of the positive aspects of linguistic interaction, those which impinge on the child, and is thus very partial and one-sided. The view of language as manners is a needless complication, in the present context, since this function of language has no counterpart in the child's experience.

Our conception of language, if it is to be adequate for meeting the needs of the child, will need to be exhaustive. It must incorporate all the child's own 'models', to take account of the varied demands on language that he himself makes. The child's understanding of what language is is derived from his own experience of language in situations of use. It thus embodies all of the images we have described: the instrumental, the regulatory, the interactional, the personal, the heuristic, the imaginative and the representational. Each of these is his interpretation of a function of language with which he is familiar. Doughty has shown, in a very suggestive paper, how different concepts of the role of the English teacher tend to incorporate and to emphasize different functions, or groups of functions, from among those here enumerated.

*   *   *

Let us summarize the models in terms of the child's intentions, since different uses of language may be seen as realizing different intentions. In its instrumental function, language is used for the satisfaction of material needs; this is the 'I want' function. The regulatory is the 'do as I tell you' function, language in the control of behaviour. The interactional function is that of getting along with others, the 'me and you' function (including 'me and my mummy'). The personal is related to this: it is the expression of identity, of the self, which develops largely *through* linguistic interaction; the 'here I come' function, perhaps. The heuristic is the use of language to learn, to explore reality: the function of 'tell me why'. The imaginative is that of 'let's pretend', whereby the reality is created, and what is being explored is the child's own mind, including language itself. The representational is the 'I've got something to tell you' function, that of the communication of content.

What we have called 'models' are the images that we have of language arising out of these functions. Language is 'defined' for the child by its uses; it is something that serves this set of needs. These are not models of language acquisition; they are not procedures whereby the child learns his language, nor do they define the part played by different types of linguistic activity in the

9

learning process. Hence no mention has been made of the chanting and repeating and rehearsing by which the child practises his language. The techniques of mastering language do not constitute a 'use', nor do they enter into the making of the image of language; a child, at least, does not learn for the luxury of being a learner. For the child, all language is doing something: in other words, it has meaning. It has meaning in a very broad sense, including here a range of functions which the adult does not normally think of as meaningful, such as the personal and the interactional and probably most of those listed above—all except the last, in fact. But it is precisely in relation to the child's conception of language that it is most vital for us to redefine our notion of meaning; not restricting it to the narrow limits of representational meaning (that is, 'content') but including within it all the functions that language has as purposive, non-random, contextualized activity.

Bernstein has shown that educational failure is often, in a very general and rather deep sense, language failure. The child who does not succeed in the school system may be one who is not using language in the ways required by the school. In its simplest interpretation, this might seem to mean merely that the child cannot read or write or express himself adequately in speech. But these are as it were the externals of linguistic success, and it is likely that underlying the failure to master these skills is a deeper and more general problem, a fundamental mismatch between the child's linguistic capabilities and the demands that are made upon them.

This is not a lack of words; vocabulary seems to be learnt very easily in response to opportunity combined with motivation. Nor is it, in any sense, an impoverishment of the grammar: there is no real evidence to show that the unsuccessful child uses or disposes of a narrower range of syntactic options. (I hope it is unnecessary to add that it has also nothing to do with dialect or accent.) Rather it would appear that the child who, in Bernstein's terms, has only a 'restricted code' suffers some limitation in respect of the set of linguistic models that we have outlined above, because some of the functions of language have been developed one-sidedly. The 'restriction' is a restriction on the range of uses of language. In particular, he may not make unrestricted use of his linguistic resources in the two functions which are most crucial to his success in school: the personal function, and the heuristic function.

In order to be taught successfully, it is necessary to know how to use language to learn; and also, how to use language to participate *as an individual* in the learning situation. These requirements may

10

be a feature of a particular kind of educational system, or they may be inherent in the very concept of education. The ability to operate institutionally in the personal and heuristic modes is, however, something that has to be learnt; it does not follow automatically from the acquisition of the grammar and vocabulary of the mother tongue. It is not, that is to say, a question of which words and structures the child knows or uses, but of their functional significance and interpretation. In Bernstein's formulation, the child may not be oriented towards the types of meaning embodied in these uses of language in certain contexts. Restricted and elaborated code are in effect, as Ruqaiya Hasan suggests, principles of semantic organization, determining the meanings that the syntactic patterns and the lexical items have for the child who hears or uses them.

To say that educational failure is linguistic failure is merely to take the first step in explaining it: it means that the most immediately accessible cause of educational failure is to be sought in language. Beyond this, and underlying the linguistic failure, is a complex pattern of social and familial factors whose significance has been revealed by Bernstein's work. But while the limitations of a child's linguistic experience may ultimately be ascribed—though not in any simple or obvious way—to features of the social background, the problem as it faces the teacher is essentially a linguistic problem. It is a limitation on the child's control over the relevant functions of language in their adaptation to certain specific demands. Whether one calls it a failure in language or a failure in the use of language is immaterial; the distinction between knowing language and knowing how to use it is merely one of terminology. This situation is not easy even to diagnose; it is much more difficult to treat. We have tried here to shed some light on it by relating it to the total set of demands, in terms of the needs of the child, that language is called upon to serve.

The implication for a teacher is that his own model of language should at least not fall short of that of the child. If the teacher's image of language is narrower and less rich than that which is already present in the minds of those he is teaching (or which needs to be present, if they are to succeed), it will be irrelevant to him as a teacher. A minimum requirement for an educationally relevant approach to language is that it takes account of the child's own linguistic experience, defining this experience in terms of its richest potential and noting where there may be differences of orientation which could cause certain children difficulties in

11

school. This is one component. The other component of relevance is the relevance to the experiences that the child will have later on: to the linguistic demands that society will eventually make on him, and, in the intermediate stage, to the demands on language which the school is going to make and which he must meet if he is to succeed in the classroom.

We are still very ignorant of many aspects of the part language plays in our lives. But it is clear that language serves a wide range of human needs, and the richness and variety of its functions is reflected in the nature of language itself, in its organization as a system: within the grammatical structure of a language, certain areas are primarily associated with the heuristic and representational functions, others with the personal and interactional functions. Different bits of the system, as it were, do different jobs; and this in turn helps us to interpret and make more precise the notion of uses of language. What is common to every use of language is that it is meaningful, contextualized, and in the broadest sense social; this is brought home very clearly to the child, in the course of his day-to-day experience. The child is surrounded by language, but not in the form of grammars and dictionaries, or of randomly chosen words and sentences, of or undirected monologue. What he encounters is 'text', or language in use: sequences of language articulated each within itself and with the situation in which it occurs. Such sequences are purposive—though very varied in purpose—and have an evident social significance. The child's awareness of language cannot be isolated from his awareness of language function, and this conceptual unity offers a useful vantage point from which language may be seen in a perspective that is educationally relevant.

The original version of this paper was presented to a conference of teachers in Approved Schools organized by the Home Office Children's Department Development Group and the Schools Council Programme in Linguistics and English Teaching at Sunningdale, May 1969. A revised version was published in the *Educational Review*, November 1969.

REFERENCES

Bernstein, Basil (1971). *Class, Codes and Control 1: theoretical studies towards a sociology of language* (Routledge & Kegan Paul, London series: Primary Socialization, Language and Education). [esp. Chapters 9 and 10]

Doughty, Peter, Pearce, John and Thornton, Geoffrey (1972). *Exploring*

Language (Edward Arnold, London Schools Council Programme in Linguistics and English Teaching). [esp. Chapters 1, 3 and 7]

Halliday, M. A. K., McIntosh, Angus and Strevens, Peter (1964). *The Linguistic Sciences and Language Teaching* (Longman, London (Longman Linguistics Library)). [esp. Chapter 4]

Hasan, Ruqaiya (1972). 'Code, register and social dialect', in Basil Bernstein (ed.), *Class, Codes and Control 2: applied studies towards a sociology of language* (Routledge & Kegan Paul, London series: Primary Socialization, Language and Education).

Mackay, David, Thompson, Brian and Schaub, Pamela (1970). *Breakthrough to Literacy: Teachers' Manual* (Longmans, ¦London Schools Council Programme in Linguistics and English Teaching).

Turner, Geoffrey J. 'Social class and children's language of control at age five and age seven, in Bernstein (ed.), *Class, Codes and Control 2* [see Hasan, above].

2 The functional basis of language

What do we understand by a 'functional approach' to the study of language? Investigations into 'the functions of language' have often figured prominently in linguistic research; there are several possible reasons for wanting to gain some insight into how language is used. Among other things, it would be helpful to be able to establish some general principles relating to the use of language; and this is perhaps the most usual interpretation of the concept of a functional approach.

But another question, no less significant, is that of the relation between the functions of language and language itself. If language has evolved in the service of certain functions, that may in the broadest sense be called 'social' functions, has this left its mark? Has the character of language been shaped and determined by what we use it for? There are a number of reasons for suggesting that it has; and, if this is true, then it may be an important factor in any discussion of language and society.

There is one aspect of the relation between language and its use which immediately springs to mind, but which is not the one we are concerned with here. The social functions of language clearly determine the pattern of language *varieties*, in the sense of what have been called 'diatypic' varieties, or 'registers'; the register range, or linguistic repertoire, of a community or of an individual is derived from the range of uses that language is put to in that particular culture or sub-culture. There will probably be no bureaucratic mode of discourse in a society without a bureaucracy. The concept 'range of uses' has to be understood carefully and with common sense: there might well, for example, be a register of military diction in a hypothetical society that does not make war—because it observes and records the exploits of others that do. Its uses of language do not include fighting, but they do

14

include historiography and news reporting. This is not a departure from the principle, merely an indication that it must be thought-fully applied.[1]

But diatypic variation in language, the existence of different fields and modes and tenors of discourse, is part of the resources of the linguistic system; and the system has to be able to accommodate it. If we are able to vary our level of formality in talking or writing, or to switch freely between one type of context and another, using language now to plan some organized activity, now to deliver a public lecture, now to keep the children in order, this is because the nature of language is such that it has all these functions built in to its total capacity. So even if we start from a consideration of how language varies—how we make different selections in meaning, and therefore in grammar and vocabulary, according to the context of use—we are led into the more fundamental question of the relation between the functions of language and the nature of the linguistic system.

Hence the interpretation of our original question which concerns us here is this: Is the social functioning of language reflected in linguistic structure—that is, in the internal organization of language as a system? It is not unreasonable to expect that it will be. It was said to be, in fact, by Malinowski, who wrote in 1923 that 'language in its structure mirrors the real categories derived from the practical attitudes of the child . . .'.[2] In Malinowski's view all uses of language, throughout all stages of cultural evolution, had left their imprint on linguistic structure, although 'if our theory is right, the fundamental outlines of grammar are due mainly to the most primitive uses of language'.

It was in the language of young children that Malinowski saw most clearly the functional origins of the language system. His formulation was, actually, 'the practical attitudes of the child, and of primitive or natural man'; but he later modified this view, realizing that linguistic research had demonstrated that there was no such thing as a 'primitive language'—all adult speech represented the same highly sophisticated level of linguistic evolution. Similarly all uses of language, however abstract, and however complex the social structure with which they were associated, were to be explained in terms of certain very elementary functions. It may be true that the developing language system of the child in some sense traverses, or at least provides an analogy for, the stages through which language itself has evolved; but there are no living specimens of its ancestral types, so that any evidence can only

15

come from within, from studying the language system and how it is learnt by a child.

Malinowski's ideas were rather ahead of his time, and they were not yet backed up by adequate investigations of language development. Not that there was no important work available in this field at the time Malinowski was writing; there was, although the first great expansion of interest came shortly afterwards. But most of the work—and this remained true until very recently, right throughout the second wave of expansion, the psycholinguistic movement of the 1960's—was concerned primarily with the mechanism of language rather than with its meaning and function. On the one hand, the interest lay in the acquisition of sounds: in the control of the means of articulation and, later on, in the mastery of the sound system, the phonology, of the language in question. On the other hand, attention was focused on the acquisition of linguistic forms: the vocabulary and the grammar of the mother tongue. The earlier studies along these lines were mainly concerned with the learning of words and word-grammar —the size of the child's vocabulary month by month, and the relative frequency of the different parts of speech—backed up by investigations of his control of sentence syntax in the written medium.[3] More recently the emphasis has tended to shift towards the acquisition of linguistic structures, seen in terms of a particular psycholinguistic view (the so-called 'nativist' view) of the language-learning faculty.

These represent different models of, or orientations towards, the language-learning process. They are not, however, either singly or collectively, adequate or particularly relevant to our present perspective. For this purpose, language acquisition, or rather language development to revert to the earlier term 'acquisition' is a rather misleading metaphor, suggesting that language is some sort of property to be owned—needs to be seen as the mastery of linguistic functions. Learning one's mother tongue is learning the uses of language, and the meanings, or rather the meaning potential, associated with them. The structures, the words and the sounds are the realization of this meaning potential. Learning language is learning how to mean.

If language development is regarded as the development of a meaning potential it becomes possible to consider the Malinowskian thesis seriously, since we can begin by looking at the relation between the child's linguistic structures and the uses he is putting language to. Let us do so in a moment. First, however,

16

we should raise the question of what we mean by putting language to this or that use, what the notion of language as serving certain functions really implies. What are 'social functions of language', in the life of *homo grammaticus*, the talking ape?

One way of leading into this question is to consider certain very specialized uses of language. The languages of games furnish many such instances; for example, the bidding system of contract bridge. The language of bidding may be thought of as a system of meaning potential, a range of options that are open to the player as performer (speaker) and as receiver (addressee). The potential is shared; it is neutral as between speaker and hearer, but it presupposes speaker, hearer and situation. It is a linguistic system: there is a set of options, and this provides an environment for each option in terms of the others—the system includes not merely the option of saying 'four hearts' but also the specification of when it is appropriate. The ability to say 'four hearts' in the right place, which is an instance, albeit a trivial one, of what Hymes explains as 'communicative competence', is sometimes thought of as if it was something quite separate from the ability to say 'four hearts' at all; but this is an artificial the distinction: there are merely different contexts, and the meaning of four hearts within the context of the bidding stage of a game of contract bridge is different from its meaning elsewhere. (We are not concerned, of course, with whether four hearts is 'a good bid' in the circumstances or not, since this cannot be expressed in terms of the system. We are concerned, however, with the fact that 'four hearts' is meaningful in the game following 'three no trumps' or 'four diamonds' but not following 'four spades'.) We are likely to find ourselves entangled in this problem, of trying to force a distinction between meaning and function, if we insist on characterizing language subjectively as the ability, or competence, of the speaker, instead of objectively as a potential, a set of alternatives. Hence my preference for the concept of 'meaning potential', which is what the speaker/hearer *can* (what he can mean, if you like), not what he knows. The two are, to an extent, different ways of looking at the same thing; but the former, 'inter-organism' perspective has different implications from the latter, 'intra-organism' one.

There are many 'restricted languages' of this kind, in games, systems of greetings, musical scores, weather reports, recipes and numerous other such generalized contexts. The simplest instance is one in which the text consists of only one message unit, or a string of message units linked by 'and'; a well-known example is the set of a hundred or so cabled messages that one was permitted to send home at one time while on active service, a typical expression being *61 & 92*, decoded perhaps as 'happy birthday and please send DDT'. Here the meaning potential is simply the list of possible messages, as a set of options, together with the option of choosing more than once, perhaps with some specified maximum length.

The daily life of the individual talking ape does not revolve around options like these, although much of his speech does take place in fairly restricted contexts where the options are limited and the meaning potential is, in fact, rather closely specifiable. Buying and selling in a shop, going to the doctor, and many of the routines of the working day all represent situation types in which the language is by no means restricted as a whole, the transactional meanings are not closed, but nevertheless there are certain definable patterns, certain options which typically come into play. Of course one can indulge in small talk with the doctor, just as one can chatter idly while bidding at bridge; these non-transactional instances of language use (or, better, 'extra-contextual', since 'transactional' is too narrow—the talk about the weather which accompanies certain social activities is not strictly transactional, but it is clearly functional within the context) do not at all disturb the point. To say this is no more than to point out that the fact that a teacher can behave with his students otherwise than in his contextual role as a teacher does not contradict the existence of a teacher–student relationship in the social structure. Conversation on the telephone does not constitute a social context, but the entry and the closure both do: there are prescribed ways of beginning and ending the conversation.[4] All these examples relate to delimitable contexts, to social functions of language; they illustrate what we use language for, and what we expect to achieve by means of language that we should not achieve without it. It is instructive here to think of various more or less everyday tasks and ask oneself how much more complicated they would be to carry out if we had to do so without the aid of language.[5]

We could try to write a list of 'uses of language' that we would expect to be typical of an educated adult member of society. But such a list could be indefinitely prolonged, and would not by itself tell us very much. When we talk of 'social functions of language', we mean those contexts which are significant in that we are able to specify some of the meaning potential that is

18

characteristically, and explainably, associated with them. And we shall be particularly interested if we find that in doing so we can throw light on certain features in the internal organization of language.

With this in mind, let us now go on to consider the language of the child, and in particular the relation between the child's linguistic structures and the uses to which he puts his language. The language system of the very young child is, effectively, a set of restricted language varieties; and it is characteristic of young children's language that its internal form reflects rather directly the function that it is being used to serve. What the child does with language tends to determine its structure. This relatively close match between structure and function can be brought out by a functional analysis of the system, in terms of its meaning potential. We can see from this how the structures that the child has mastered are direct reflections of the functions that language serves for him.

Figures 1–3 give an actual example of the language system of a small child. They are taken from the description of Nigel's language at age 19 months; and each represents one functional component of the system—or rather, each one represents just a part of one such component, to keep the illustration down to a reasonable size. The total system is made up of five or six functional components of this kind.[6] Figure 1 shows the system Nigel has developed for the instrumental function of language. This refers to the use of language for the purpose of satisfying material needs: it is the 'I want' function, including of course 'I don't want'. Here the child has developed a meaning potential in which he can request either goods or services, the latter in the form either of physical assistance or of having something made available to him. We show some examples of these requests. In addition his demand may be in response to a question 'do you want . . . ?', in which case the answer may be positive or negative; or it may be initiated by himself, in which case it is always positive. Furthermore under one set of conditions, namely where the demand is initiated by himself and it is a demand for a specific item of food, there is a further option in the meaning potential since he has learnt that he can demand not only a first instalment but also a supplementary one, 'more'. (This does not correspond to the adult interpretation; he may ask for more bread when he has not yet had any bread but has had something else. Note that he has not yet learnt the meaning 'no more'.) With toiletry, and with

19

Nigel at 19 months: part of the instrumental component

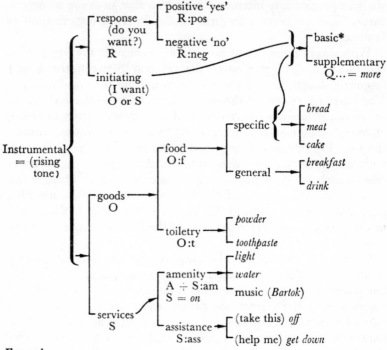

Examples:

yes	no	bread	breakfast	more bread	powder	water on	Bartok on
R:pos	R:neg	O:f	O:f	Q + O:f	O:t	A + S:am	A + S:am
ʔē	nó	bɹiɛ	bɹɛka	mɔ̄ bɹɛ	bʷga	wɔta ʔɔn	tābɔ̄ ʔɔn
yes I want it	no I don't want it	I want some bread	I want my breakfast	I want some more bread	I want some powder	I want the water tap turned on	I want a record put on

off	get down
S:ass	S:ass
ʔɔfva	dƔkao
I want my bib taken off	I want to get down

Elements:
O object of desire [food, toiletry]
S service [amenity, assistance]
R response [positive, negative]
Q quantifier
A amenity

Figure 1

20

general demands for food, this option does not arise. In the system of 'basic' versus 'supplementary', therefore, the term 'basic' is the unmarked one (indicated by the asterisk), where 'unmarked' is defined as that which must be selected if the conditions permitting a choice are not satisfied.

Each option in the meaning potential is expressed, or 'realized', by some structure-forming element. In the instrumental component there are just five of these: the response element, the object of desire, the service desired, the amenity and the quantifier. The selection which the child makes of a particular configuration of options within his meaning potential is organized as a structure; but it is a structure in which the elements are very clearly related to the type of function which the language is being made to serve for him. For example, there is obviously a connection between the 'instrumental' function of language and the presence, in the structures derived from it, of an element having the structural function 'object of desire'. What is significant is not, of course, the label we put on it, but the fact that we are led to identify a particular category, to which a label such as this then turns out to be appropriate.

The analysis that we have offered is a functional one in the two distinct but related senses in which the term 'functional' is used in linguistics. It is an account of the functions of language; and at the same time the structures are expressed in terms of functional elements (and not of classes, such as noun and verb). It could be thought of as a kind of 'case grammar', although the structural parts are strictly speaking 'elements of structure' (as in system-structure theory) rather than 'cases'; they are specific to the context (i.e. to the particular function of language, in this instance), and they account for the entire structure, whereas cases are contextually undifferentiated and also restricted to elements that are syntactically dependent on a verb.

We have assumed for purposes of illustration a relatively early stage of language learning; at this stage Nigel has only one- and two-element structures. But it does not matter much which stage was chosen; the emphasis is here on the form of the language system. This consists of a meaning potential, represented as a network of options, which are derived from a particular social function and are realized, in their turn, by structures whose elements relate directly to the meanings that are being expressed. These elements seem to be more appropriately described in terms such as 'object of desire', which clearly derives from the 'I want'

Nigel at 19 months: part of the regulatory component

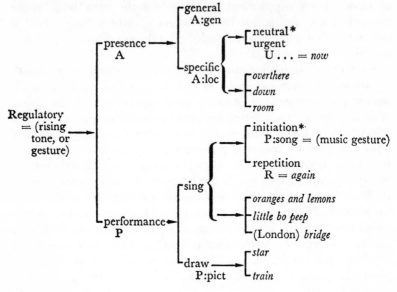

Examples:

come	overthere	down	now overthere	now room	star	train
A:gen	A:loc ⤹	A:loc	U + A:loc⤸	U + A:loc	P:pict	P:pict
kĕm	ɔ́uvədɛ̀ə	daú	naū ɔ́uvədɛ̀ə	naū ɹɷ̄m	dá	tɣɷ̄fa
follow	come over	come (&	come over	come into	draw a	draw a
me	there	sit) down	there with me	your room	star	train
	with me	with me	at once	with me		
				at once		

oranges-&-lemons   again

P:song   R

ɔɹʷelèmə   agǣi

sing 'oranges   sing that
and lemons'   again
[accompanied
by music gesture]

Elements:
A   accompany [general, locational]
P   perform [song, picture]
U   urgency
R   repetition

Figure 2

22

function of language, than in any 'purely' grammatical terms, whether these are drawn from the grammar of the adult language (like 'subject') or introduced especially to account for the linguistic structures of the child (like 'pivot'). I shall suggest, however, that in principle the same is true of the elements of structure of the adult language: that these also have their origin in the social functions of language, though in a way that is less direct and therefore less immediately apparent. Even such a 'purely grammatical' function as 'subject' is derivable from language in use; in fact the notion that there are 'purely grammatical' elements of structure is really self-contradictory.

The same principle is noticeable in the other two functions which we are illustrating here, again in a simplified form. One of these is the 'regulatory' function of language (Figure 2). This is the use of language to control the behaviour of others, to manipulate the persons in the environment; the 'do as I tell you' function. Here we find a basic distinction between a demand for the other person's company and a demand for a specific action on his or her part. The demand for company may be a general request to 'come with me', or refer to a particular location 'over there', 'down here', 'in the (other) room'; and it may be marked for urgency. The performance requested may be drawing a picture or singing a song; if it is a song, it may be new (for the occasion) or a repeat performance. It is interesting to note that there is no negative in the regulatory function at this stage; the meaning 'prohibition' is not among the options in the child's potential.

The third example is of the 'interactional' function (Figure 3). This is the child's use of language as a means of personal interaction with those around him; the 'me and you' function of language. Here the child is either interacting with someone who is present ('greeting') or seeking to interact with someone who is absent ('calling'). That someone may either be generalized, with *hullo* used (i) in narrow tone accompanied by a smile, to commune with an intimate or greet a stranger, or (ii) in wide tone, loud, to summon company; or it may be personalized, in which case it is either a statement of the need for interaction, . . . *come!*, or a search, *where . . . ?* And there is here a further choice in meaning, realized by intonation. All utterances in the instrumental and regulatory functions end on a high rising tone, unless this is replaced by a gesture, as in the demand for music; this is the tone which is used when the child requires a response of any kind. In the interactional function there are two types of utterance, those

23

requiring a response and those not; the former have the final rise, the latter end on a falling tone (as do utterances in the other functions which we have not illustrated here).

Nigel at 19 months: part of the interactional component

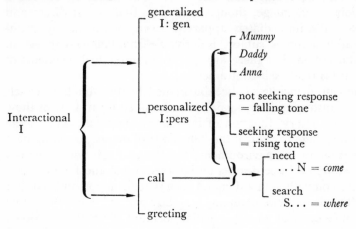

Examples:

hullo	hullo	Mummy	Anna	Mummy come	Anna come	where Daddy
I:gen	I:gen	I:pers	I:pers	I:pers + N	I:pers + N	S + I:pers
ɛlɔ̄uwȁ	ɛlɔ̄uwá	mɛ̄mȉ	āná	mɛ̄mȉ kɛ̀m	ānā kɛ́m	wɛə dādȁ
hullo!	hullo?	Mummy!	Anna?	Mummy. I	Anna where	I'm looking
(greeting)	who's	here	where	want you.	are you?	for Daddy
[narrow	there?	you	are		I want	
tone; +	(call)	are!	you?		you.	
smile]	[wide					
	tone]					

where Mummy

S + I:pers

wɛə mɛmi

I want to
know where
Mummy is

Elements:

I interaction [general, personal]
N need
S search

Figure 3

It would be wrong to draw too sharp a line between the different functions in the child's linguistic system. There is a clear connection between the instrumental and the regulatory functions, in that both represent types of demand to be met by

24

some action on the part of the addressee; and between the regulatory and the interactional, in that both involve the assumption of an interpersonal relationship. Nevertheless the functions we have suggested are distinguishable from one another; and this is important, because it is through the gradual extension of his meaning potential into new functions that the child's linguistic horizons become enlarged. In the instrumental function, it does not matter who provides the bread or turns the tap on; the intention is satisfied by the provision of the object or service in question. In the regulatory function on the other hand the request involves a specific person; it is he and no one else who must respond, by his behaviour. The interactional also involves a specific person; but he is not being required to do anything, merely to be there and in touch. There are, to be sure, borderline cases, and there are overlaps in the realization (e.g. *come* is sometimes regulatory, sometimes interactional in meaning); but such indeterminacy will be found in any system of this kind.

These extracts from the account of Nigel's developing linguistic system will serve to illustrate the types of structure that are encountered in the language of the very young child, and how they relate directly to the options that he has in his meaning potential. The networks show what the child can do, in the sense of what he can mean; the structural interpretations show the mechanism by which he does it—how the meanings are expressed, through configurations of elementary functions.

In the first paper I suggested what seem to me to be the basic functions that language comes to fulfil in the early life of the child. These are the generalized social functions of language in the context of the young child's life. When the child has learnt to use language to some extent in any of these functions, however limited the grammatical and lexical resources he can bring to bear, then he has built up a meaning potential for that function and has mastered at least a minimal structural requirement—it may be a 'configuration' of only one element—for purposes of expressing it.

The social functions which language is serving in the life of the child determine both the options which he creates for himself and their realizations in structure. We see this clearly in the language of young children, once we begin to think of language development as the development of the social functions of language and of a meaning potential associated with them. However, although this connection between the functions of language and the linguistic system is clearest in the case of the language of very young children, it is essentially, I think, a feature of language as a whole. The internal organization of natural language can best be explained in the light of the social functions which language has evolved to serve. Language is as it is because of what it has to do. Only, the relation between language function and language structure will appear less directly, and in more complex ways, in the fully developed adult system than in children's language.

To say this is in effect to claim, with Malinowski, that ontogeny does in some respect provide a model for phylogeny. We cannot examine the origins of language. But if we can relate the form of the adult language system to its social functions, and at the same time show that the language of the child, in its various stages, is explainable in terms of the uses that he has mastered up to the particular stage, then we have at least opened up the possibility of interesting discussion about the nature and social origins of language.

*　　　　*　　　　*

It is characteristic, it seems, of the utterances of the very young child that they are functionally simple; each utterance serves just one function. If an utterance is instrumental in function, seeking the satisfaction of some material desire, then it is just instrumental and nothing else. This represents a very early stage of language development. It is shown in our illustrations by the fact that each utterance is totally specified by just one network: to derive *more bread*! we need only the instrumental system network, which fully describes its structure.

The adult language bears the marks of its humble origins in systems like these. But it differs in fundamental ways; and perhaps the most fundamental—because this is what makes it necessary to develop a level of linguistic form (grammar and vocabulary) intermediate between meanings and sounds—is the fact that utterances in the adult language are functionally complex. Every adult linguistic act, with a few broadly specifiable exceptions, is serving more than one function at once.

One very familiar type of phenomenon which illustrates this fact is that of denotation and connotation in word meanings. For example, after the F.A. Cup Final match between Leeds and Chelsea, a friend of mine who is a Londoner greeted me with *I see Chelsea trounced Leeds again*, using the word *trounce* which means 'defeat' plus 'I am pleased'. But the functional multivalence of this utterance goes much further than is signalled by the word-meaning of *trounce*. The speaker was conveying a piece of information, which he suspected I already possessed, together with the further information (which I did not possess) that he also possessed it; he was referring it to our shared experience; expressing his triumph over me (I am a Leeds supporter and he knows it); and relating back to some previous exchanges between us. There is no simple functional category from which we can derive this utterance, corresponding to categories such as regulatory or instrumental in the linguistic system of the young child.

The problem for a socio-linguistic theory is: what is there in the adult language which corresponds to the functional components, the systems of meaning potential, that make up the early stages in the child's language development? Or, since that is a rather slanted way of asking the question, what is the relation of the fully developed language system to the social functions of the adult language? And can we explain something of the form that languages take by examining this relation?

In one sense, the variety of social functions of language is, obviously, much greater in the adult. The adult does more different things than the child; and in a great many of his activities, he uses language. He has a very broad diatypic spectrum. Yet there is another sense in which the adult's range of functional variation may be poorer, and we can best appreciate this if we take the child as our point of departure. Among the child's uses of language there appears, after a time, the use of language to convey new information: to communicate a content that is (regarded by the speaker as) unknown to the addressee. I had referred to this in a general way as the 'representational' function; but it would be better, and also more accurate, if one were to use a more specific term, such as 'informative', since this makes it easier to interpret subsequent developments. In the course of maturation this function is increasingly emphasized, until eventually it comes to dominate, if not the adult's use of language, at least his conception of the use of language. The adult tends to be sceptical if it is suggested to him that language has other uses than that of conveying information; and he will usually think next of the use of language to *mis*inform—which is simply a variant of the informative function. Yet for the young child the informative is a rather minor function, relatively late to emerge. Many problems of communication between adult and child, for example in the infant school, arise from the adults' failure to grasp this fact. This can be seen in some adult renderings of children's rhymes and songs, which are often very dramatic, with an intonation and rhythm appropriate to the content; whereas for the child the language is not primarily content—it is language in its imaginative function, and needs to be expressed as pattern, patterns of meaning and structure and vocabulary and sound. Similarly, failures have been reported when actors have recorded foreign language courses; their renderings focus attention only on the use of language to convey information, and it seems that when learning a foreign language, as when learning the mother tongue, it is necessary to take other uses of language into account, especially in the beginning stages.

What happens in the course of maturation is a process that we might from one point of view call 'functional reduction', whereby the original functional range of the child's language—a set of fairly discrete functional components each with its own meaning potential—is gradually replaced by a more highly coded and more abstract, but also simpler, functional system. There is an immense functional diversity in the adult's use of language; immense, that is, if we simply ask 'in what kinds of activity does language play a part for him?'. But this diversity of usage is reduced in the internal organization of the adult language system—in the grammar, in other words—to a very small set of functional components. Let us call these for the moment 'macro-functions' to distinguish them from the functions of the child's emergent language system, the instrumental, the regulatory and so on. These 'macro-functions' are the highly abstract linguistic reflexes of the multiplicity of social uses of language.

The innumerable social purposes for which adults use language are not represented directly, one by one, in the form of functional components in the language system, as are those of the child. With the very young child, 'function' equals 'use'; and there is no grammar, no intermediate level of internal organization in language, only a content and an expression. With the adult, there are indefinitely many uses, but only three or four functions, or 'macro-functions' as we are calling them; and these macro-functions appear at a new level in the linguistic system—they take the form of 'grammar'. The grammatical system has as it were a functional input and a structural output; it provides the mechanism for different functions to be combined in one utterance in the way the adult requires. But these macro-functions, although they are only indirectly related to specific uses of language, are still recognizable as abstract representations of the basic functions which language is made to serve.

One of these macro-functions is what is sometimes called the representational one. But just as earlier, in talking of the use of language to convey information, I preferred the more specific term 'informative', so here I shall also prefer another term—but this time a different one, because this is a very distinct concept. Here we are referring to the linguistic expression of ideational content; let us call this macro-function of the adult language system the 'ideational' function. For the child, the use of language to inform is just one instance of language use, one function among many. But with the adult, the ideational element in language is present in all its uses; no matter what he is doing with language he will find himself exploiting its ideational resources, its potential for expressing a content in terms of the speaker's experience and that of the speech community. There are exceptions, types of utterance like *how do you do?* and *no wonder!* which have no ideational content in them; but otherwise there is some ideational component involved, however small, in all the specific uses of language in which the adult typically engages.

This no doubt is why the adult tends to think of language primarily in terms of its capacity to inform. But where is the origin of this ideational element to be sought within the linguistic repertoire of the very young child? Not, I think, in the informative function, which seems to be in some sense secondary, derived from others that have already appeared. It is to be sought rather in the combination of the personal and the heuristic, in that phase of linguistic development which becomes crucial at a particular time, probably (as in Nigel's case) shortly after the emergence of the more directly pragmatic functions which we illustrated in Figures 1–3. At the age from which these examples were taken, 19 months, Nigel had already begun to use language also in the personal, the heuristic and the imaginative functions; it was noticeable that language was becoming, for him, a means of organizing and storing his experience. Here we saw the beginnings of a 'grammar'—that is, a level of lexicogrammatical organization, or linguistic 'form'; and of utterances having more than one function. The words and structures learnt in these new functions were soon turned also to pragmatic use, as in some of the examples quoted of the instrumental and regulatory functions. But it appears that much of the initial impetus to the learning of the formal patterns (as distinct from the spontaneous modes of expression characteristic of the first few months of speech) was the need to impose order on the environment and to define his own person in relation to and in distinction from it. Hence—to illustrate just from vocabulary—we find the word *bus*, though it is RECOGNIZED as the name of a toy bus as well as of full-sized specimens, being used at first exclusively to comment on the sight or sound of buses in the street and only later as a demand for the toy; and the one or two exceptions to this, e.g. *bird* which was at first used ONLY in the instrumental sense of 'I want my toy bird', tend to drop out of the system altogether and are relearnt in a personal-heuristic context later.

It seems therefore that the personal-heuristic function is a major impetus to the enlarging of the ideational element in the child's linguistic system. We should not however exaggerate its role vis-à-vis that of the earlier pragmatic functions; the period 15–21 months was in Nigel's case characterized by a rapid development of grammatical and lexical resources which were (as a whole) exploited in all the functional contexts that he had mastered so far. The one function that had not yet emerged was the informative; even when pressed—as he frequently was—to 'tell Mummy where you went' or 'tell Daddy what you saw', he was incapable of doing so, although in many instances he had previously used the required sentences quite appropriately in a different function. It was clear that he had not internalized the fact that language could be used to tell people things they did not know, to communicate experience that had NOT been shared. But this was no barrier to the development of an ideational component in his linguistic system. The ideational element, as it evolves, becomes crucial to the use of language in all the functions that the child has learnt to control; and this gives the clue to its status as a 'macro-function'. Whatever specific use one is making of language, one will sooner or later find it necessary to refer explicitly to the categories of one's experience of the world. All, or nearly all, utterances come to have an ideational component in them. But, at the same time, they all have something else besides.

When we talk of the ideational function of the adult language, therefore, we are using 'function' in a more generalized sense (as indicated by our term 'macro-function') than when we refer to the specific functions that make up the language of the young child. Functions such as 'instrumental' and 'regulatory' are really the same thing as 'uses of language'. The ideational function, on the

30

other hand, is a major component of meaning in the language system that is basic to more or less all uses of language. It is still a 'meaning potential', although the potential is very vast and complex; for example, the whole of the transitivity system in language—the interpretation and expression in language of the different types of process of the external world, including material, mental and abstract processes of every kind—is part of the ideational component of the grammar. And the structures that express these ideational meanings are still recognizably derived from the meanings themselves; their elements are in this respect not essentially different from those such as 'object of desire' that we saw in Figures 1–3. They represent the categories of our interpretation of experience. So for example a clause such as *Sir Christopher Wren built this gazebo* may be analysed as a configuration of the functions 'agent' *Sir Christopher Wren*, 'process: material: creation' *built*, 'goal: effected' *this gazebo*, where 'agent', 'process', 'goal' and their sub-categories reflect our understanding of phenomena that come within our experience. Hence this function of language, which is that of encoding our experience in the form of an ideational content, not only specifies the available options in meaning but also determines the nature of their structural realizations. The notions of agent, process and the like make sense only if we assume an ideational function in the adult language, just as 'object of desire' and 'service' make sense only if we assume an instrumental function in the emergent language of the child. But this analysis is not imposed from outside in order to satisfy some theory of linguistic functions; an analysis in something like these terms is necessary (whatever form it finally takes for the language in question) if we are to explain the structure of clauses. The clause is a structural unit, and it is the one by which we express a particular range of ideational meanings, our experience of processes—the processes of the external world, both concrete and abstract, and the processes of our own consciousness, seeing, liking, thinking, talking and so on. Transitivity is simply the grammar of the clause in its ideational aspect.

Figure 4 sets out the principal options in the transitivity system of English, showing how these are realized in the form of structures. It can be seen that the structure-forming elements—agent, process, phenomenon etc.—are all related to the general function of expressing processes. The labels that we give to them describe their specific roles in the encoding of these meanings, but the elements themselves are identified syntactically. Thus in the

Summary of principal options in the English clause (simplified; structural indices for transitivity only)

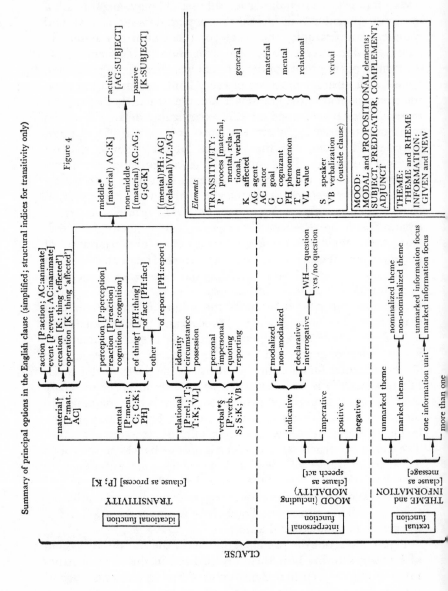

Figure 4

32

English clause there is a distinct element of structure which expresses the cause of a process when that process is brought about by something other than the entity that is primarily affected by it (e.g. *the storm* in *the storm shook the house*); we can reasonably label this the 'agent', but whether we do so or not it is present in the grammar, as an element deriving from the ideational function of language.

The clause, however, is not confined to the expression of transitivity; it has other functions besides. There are non-ideational elements in the adult language system, even though the adult speaker is often reluctant to recognize them. Again, however, they are grouped together as a single 'macro-function' in the grammar, covering a whole range of particular uses of language. This is the macro-function that we shall refer to as the 'interpersonal'; it embodies all use of language to express social and personal relations, including all forms of the speaker's intrusion into the speech situation and the speech act. The young child also uses language interpersonally, as we have seen, interacting with other people, controlling their behaviour, and also expressing his own personality and his own attitudes and feelings; but these uses are specific and differentiated. Later on they become generalized in a single functional component of the grammatical system, at this more abstract level. In the clause, the interpersonal element is represented by mood and modality: the selection by the speaker of a particular role in the speech situation, and his determination of the choice of roles for the addressee (mood), and the expression of his judgments and predictions (modality).

We are not suggesting that one cannot distinguish, in the adult language, specific uses of language of a socio-personal kind; on the contrary, we can recognize an unlimited number. We use language to approve and disapprove; to express belief, opinion, doubt; to include in the social group, or exclude from it; to ask and answer; to express personal feelings; to achieve intimacy; to greet, chat up, take leave of; in all these and many other ways. But in the structure of the adult language there is an integrated 'interpersonal' component, which provides the meaning potential for this element as it is present in all uses of language, just as the 'ideational' component provides the resources for the representation of experience that is also an essential element whatever the specific type of language use.

These two macro-functions, the ideational and the interpersonal, together determine a large part of the meaning potential

33

that is incorporated in the grammar of every language. This can be seen very clearly in the grammar of the clause, which has its ideational aspect, transitivity, and its interpersonal aspect, mood (including modality), There is also a third macro-function, the 'textual', which fills the requirement that language should be operationally relevant—that it should have a texture, in real contexts of situation, that distinguishes a living message from a mere entry in a grammar or a dictionary. This third component provides the remaining strands of meaning potential to be woven into the fabric of linguistic structure.

We shall not attempt to illustrate in detail the interpersonal and the textual functions. Included in Figure 4 are a few of the principal options which make up these components in the English clause; their structural realizations are not shown, but the same principle holds, whereby the structural mechanism reflects the generalized meanings that are being expressed. The intention here is simply to bring out the fact that a linguistic structure—of which the clause is the best example—serves as a means for the integrated expression of all the functionally distinct components of meaning in language. Some simple clauses are analysed along these lines in Figure 5.

What we know as 'grammar' is the linguistic device for hooking up together the selections in meaning which are derived from the various functions of language, and realizing them in a unified structural form. Whereas with the child, in the first beginnings of the system, the functions remain unintegrated, being in effect functional varieties of speech act, with one utterance having just one function, the linguistic units of the adult language serve all (macro-) functions at once. A clause in English is the simultaneous realization of ideational, interpersonal and textual meanings. But these components are not put together in discrete fashion such that we can point to one segment of the clause as expressing one type of meaning and another segment as expressing another. The choice of a word may express one type of meaning, its morphology another and its position in sequence another; and any element is likely to have more than one structural role, like a chord in a polyphonic structure which participates simultaneously in a number of melodic lines. This last point is illustrated by the analyses in Figure 5.

We hope to have made it clear in what sense it is being said that the concept of the social function of language is central to the interpretation of language as a system. The internal organization

34

Analysis of clauses, showing simultaneous structures

	this gazebo	was	built	by Sir Christopher Wren
IDEATIONAL material: (action/creation/(non-middle: passive))	G:K: effected	P:material/action		AC:AG: animate
INTERPERSONAL declarative/non-modalized	Modal		Propositional	
	Subject	Predicator		Adjunct
TEXTUAL unmarked theme one information unit: unmarked	Theme	Rheme		
	Given		New	

	I	had		a cat . . .
IDEATIONAL relational: (possession/middle)	T:K	P:relational		VL
INTERPERSONAL declarative/non-modalized	Modal	= did	have Propositional	
	Subject	Predicator		Complement
TEXTUAL unmarked theme one information unit: unmarked	Theme	Rheme		
	Given	New		

	. . . the cat	pleased		me
ID. mental: (reaction/fact/(non-middle: active))	PH: AG: thing	P: mental: reaction		C:K
INT. declarative/non-modalized	Modal	= did	please	Propositional
	Subject	Predicator		Complement
TEXT. unmarked theme one information unit: unmarked	Theme	Rheme		
	Given	New		

	such a tale	you	would	never believe
ID. mental: (cognition/report/middle)	PH: report	C:K	P:mental: cognition	
INT. declarative/modalized negative	Propo-	Modal		-sitional
	Complement	Subject	Predicator	
TEXT. marked theme: non-nominalized two information units	Theme	Rheme		
	New	Given	New	

Figure 5

35

of language is not accidental; it embodies the functions that language has evolved to serve in the life of social man. This essentially was Malinowski's claim; and, as Malinowski suggested, we can see it most clearly in the linguistic system of the young child. There, the utterance has in principle just one structure; each element in it has therefore just one structural function, and that function is related to the meaning potential—to the set of options available to the child in that particular social function.

In the developed linguistic system of the adult, the functional origins are still discernible. Here however each utterance has a number of structures simultaneously—we have used the analogy of polyphony. Each element is a complex of roles, and enters into more than one structure (indeed the concept 'element of structure' is a purely abstract concept; it is merely a role set, which is then realized by some item in the language). The structure of the adult language still represents the functional meaning potential; but because of the variety of social uses of language, a 'grammar' has emerged whereby the options are organized into a few large sets in which the speaker selects simultaneously whatever the specific use he is making of language. These sets of options, which are recognizable empirically in the grammar, correspond to the few highly generalized realms of meaning that are essential to the social functioning of language—and hence are intrinsic to language as a system. Because language serves a generalized 'ideational' function, we are able to use it for all the specific purposes and types of context which involve the communication of experience. Because it serves a generalized 'interpersonal' function, we are able to use it for all the specific forms of personal expression and social interaction. And a prerequisite to its effective operation under both these headings is what we have referred to as the 'textual' function, whereby language becomes text, is related to itself and to its contexts of use. Without the textual component of meaning, we should be unable to make any use of language at all.

If we want to pursue this line of interpretation further, we shall have to go outside language to some theory of social meanings. From the point of view of a linguist the most important work in this field is that of Bernstein, whose theories of cultural transmission and social change are unique in this respect, that language is built into them as an essential element in social processes. Although Bernstein is primarily investigating social and not linguistic phenomena, his ideas shed very considerable light on

36

language; in particular, in relation to the concept of language as meaning potential, he has been able to define certain contexts which are crucial to the socialization of the child and to identify the significant orientations in behaviour of participants within these contexts. The behavioural options of the participants are, typically, realized through language; and with a functional interpretation of the semantic system we can begin to appreciate how it is that, in the course of expressing meanings that are specific to particular contexts of situation, language at the same time serves to transmit the essential patterns of orientation in the total context of the culture.

This provides the backdrop to a functional view of language. In front of our eyes, as it were, are the 'uses of language': we are interested in how people use language and in how language varies according to its use. Behind this lies a concern with the nature of language itself: once we interpret the notion 'uses of language' in sufficiently abstract terms we find that it gives us an insight into the way language is learnt and, through that, into the internal organization of language, why language is as it is. Behind this again is a still deeper focus, on society and the transmission of culture; for when we interpret language in these terms we may cast some light on the baffling problem of how it is that the most ordinary uses of language, in the most everyday situations, so effectively transmit the social structure, the values, the systems of knowledge, all the deepest and most pervasive patterns of the culture. With a functional perspective on language, we can begin to appreciate how this is done.

This paper was first published in *Class, Codes and Control: applied studies towards a sociology of language*, ed. Basil Bernstein (Routledge and Kegan Paul).

NOTES

1. For diatypic variety in language, see Michael Gregory, 'Aspects of varieties differentiation', *Journal of Linguistics* 3.2, 1967, 177–98. See also Jeffrey Ellis, 'On contextual meaning', in C. E. Bazell *et al.* (eds.), In Memory of J. R. Firth, London, Longman (Longman Linguistics Library), 1966.

2. Bronislaw Malinowski, 'The problem of meaning in primitive languages', Supplement 1 to C. K. Ogden and I. A. Richards, *The Meaning of Meaning*, London, Kegan Paul (International Library of Psychology, Philosophy and Scientific Method), 1923.

3. See, e.g. A. F. Watts, *The Language and Mental Development of Children* (Heath, London, 1944).

4. Emanuel A. Schegloff, *'Sequencing in conversational openings'*, 1972.

5. This was in fact a task assigned to the mothers in relation to the socialization of children in a study by Bernstein and Henderson (see Basil Bernstein and Dorothy Henderson, 'Social class differences in the relevance of language to socialization', *Sociology* 3.1, 1969, 1–20): they were asked to say how much more difficult it would be for parents who could not speak to do certain things with young children, such as disciplining them or helping them to make things. It should be borne in mind that in the present discussion we are using 'language' always to refer to the meaning potential; we assume some means of expression, but not any linguistic forms in particular.

6. The analyses given in Figures 1–3 represent a provisional interpretation of the material. For a preliminary account of early language development in functional terms see M. A. K. Halliday, 'Learning how to mean', in Eric and Elizabeth Lenneberg (eds.), *Foundations of Language Development: a multidisciplinary approach*, UNESCO & IBRO (International Brain Research Organization), forthcoming.

Summary of notational conventions

I SYSTEMS

a →[x / y]   there is a system x/y with entry condition a [if a, then either x or y]

a { →[x / y] →[m. / n] }   there are two simultaneous systems x/y and m/n, both having entry condition a [if a, then both either x or y and, independently, either m or n]

a →[x / y] x →[m / n]   there are two systems x/y and m/n, ordered in dependence such that m/n has entry condition x and x/y has entry condition a [if a then either x or y, and if x, then either m or n]

a, b } →[x / y]   there is a system x/y with compound entry condition, conjunction of a and b [if both a and b, then either x or y]

a, c } →[m / n]   there is a system m/n with two possible entry conditions, disjunction of a and c [if either a or c, or both, then either m or n]

a* ... x*   [or any paired symbol] x is unmarked with respect to a [if a, then always x]

x* x is unmarked with respect to all environments [if any tangential feature, then always x]. Note: a tangential feature is the oblique term in a superordinate system, e.g. a in   →[a / b] →[x* / y]

II STRUCTURES

X   X is added
X...   X precedes (occurs initially)
...X   X follows (occurs finally)
X + Y   Y follows X
X:z   X is (further specified as) z
X:Y   X is (combined into one element with) Y
X = a X is (realized as) a
[X]   X is optional

3 Language in a social perspective

The studies which are described in the series of monographs entitled *Primary Socialization, Language and Education*, edited by Basil Bernstein, show how in a coherent social theory a central place is occupied by language, as the primary means of cultural transmission.

What is the nature of language, when seen from this point of view? There are two sides to this question. The first is, what aspects of language are highlighted—what do we *make* language look like, so to speak—in order to understand its function in the socialization of the child, and in the processes of education? The second is the same question in reverse: what do we learn about language—what *does* it look like, in fact—when it is approached in this way?

1. Language as social behaviour an acknowledged concern of modern linguistics, and not limited to the study of instances

It has been suggested that one of the main preoccupations of the 1970's will be a concern with social man. This implies not simply man in relation to some abstract entity such as 'society as a whole' but man in relation to other men; it is a particular facet of man in relation to his environment, only it shifts the emphasis from the physical on to the human environment—on to man in the environment of men. The individual is seen as the focus of a complex of human relationships which collectively define the content of his social behaviour.

This provides a perspective on language. A significant fact about the behaviour of human beings in relation to their social environment is that a large part of it is linguistic behaviour. The study

40

of social man presupposes the study of language and social man.

A concern with language and social man has for a long time been one of the perspectives of modern linguistics. In 1935 J. R. Firth, introducing the term 'sociological linguistics', discussed the study of language in a social perspective and outlined a programme of 'describing and classifying typical contexts of situation within the context of culture . . . [and] types of linguistic function in such contexts of situation' (p. 27). We tend nowadays to refer to socio-linguistics as if this was something very different from the study of language as practised in linguistics *tout court*; but actually new 'socio-linguistics' is but old 'linguistics' writ large, and the linguist's interests have always extended to language as social behaviour.

It was Malinowski from whom Firth derived his notions of 'context of culture' and 'context of situation' (Malinowski, 1923); and Malinowski's ideas about what we might call cultural and situational semantics provide an interesting starting point for the study of language and social man, since they encourage us to look at language as a form of behaviour potential. In this definition, both the 'behaviour' and the 'potential' need to be emphasized. Language, from this point of view, is a range of possibilities, an open-ended set of options in behaviour that are available to the individual in his existence as social man. The context of culture is the environment for the total set of these options, while the context of situation is the environment of any particular selection that is made from within them.

Malinowski's two types of context thus embody the distinction between the potential and the actual. The context of culture defines the potential, the range of possibilities that are open. The actual choice among these possibilities takes place within a given context of situation.

Firth, with his interest in the actual, in the text and its relation to its surroundings, developed the notion of 'context of situation' into a valuable tool for linguistic inquiry. Firth's interest, however, was not in the accidental but in the typical: not in this or that piece of discourse that happened to get recorded in the field-worker's notebook, but in repetitive patterns which could be interpreted as significant and systematizable patterns of social behaviour. Thus, what is actual is not synonymous with what is unique, or the chance product of random observations. But the significance of what is typical—in fact the concept 'typical' itself

41

—depends on factors which lie outside language, in the social structure. It is not the typicalness of the words and structures which concerns us, but the typicalness of the context of situation, and of the function of the words and structures within it.

Malinowski (1935) tells an interesting story of an occasion when he asked his Trobriand Island informant some questions about the Trobrianders' gardening practices. He noted down the answers, and was surprised a few days later to hear the same informant repeating what he had said word for word in conversation with his young daughter. In talking to Malinowski, the informant had as it were borrowed the text from a typical context of situation. The second occasion, the discussion with the little girl, was then an instance of this context of situation in which the socialization of the child into the most significant, aspect of the material culture— the gardening practices—was a familiar process, with familiar patterns of language behaviour associated with it.

There is not, of course, any conflict between an emphasis on the repetitive character of language behaviour and an insistence on the creativity of the language system. Considered as behaviour potential, the language system itself is open-ended, since the question whether two instances are the same or not is not determined by the system; it is determined by the underlying social theory. But in any case, as Ruqaiya Hasan (1971) has pointed out, creativeness does not consist in producing new sentences. The newness of a sentence is a quite unimportant—and unascertainable—property, and 'creativity' in language lies in the speaker's ability to create new meanings: to realize the potentiality of language for the indefinite extension of its resources to new contexts of situation. It is only in this light that we can understand the otherwise unintelligible observation made by Katz and Fodor (1963), that 'almost every sentence uttered is uttered for the first time' (p. 171). Our most 'creative' acts may be precisely among those that are realized through highly repetitive forms of behaviour.

Firth did not concern himself with Malinowski's 'context of culture', since he preferred to study generalized patterns of actual behaviour, rather than attempting to characterize the potential as such. This was simply the result of his insistence on the need for accurate observations—a much-needed emphasis in the context of earlier linguistic studies—and in no way implied that the study of language could be reduced to the study of instances, which in fact he explicitly denied (1968). More to the point, Firth built his

42

linguistic theory around the original and fundamental concept of the 'system', as used by him in a technical sense; and this is precisely a means of describing the potential, and of relating the actual to it.

A 'system', as the concept was developed by Firth, can be interpreted as the set of options that is specified for a given environment. The meaning of it is 'under the conditions stated, there are the following possibilities'. By making use of this notion, we can describe language in the form of a behaviour potential. In this way the analysis of language comes within the range of a social theory, provided the underlying concepts of such a theory are such that they can be shown to be realized in social context and patterns of behaviour.

The interest in language and social man is thus no new theme in linguistics. It is also predominant in the important work of Pike (1967, first published 1954–60). Its scope is not limited to the description of individual acts of speech; more significant has been the attempt to relate grammatical and lexical features, and combinations of such features, to types of social interaction and, where possible, to generalized social concepts. From a sociological point of view it would be of no interest otherwise; a social theory could not operate with raw speech fragments as the only linguistic exponents of its fundamental ideas.

2. Language in a social perspective interpreted through the concept of 'meaning potential'

If we regard language as social behaviour, therefore, this means that we are treating it as a form of behaviour *potential*. It is what the speaker can do.

But 'can do' by itself is not a linguistic notion; it encompasses types of behaviour other than language behaviour. If we are to relate the notion of 'can do' to the sentences and words and phrases that the speaker is able to construct in his language—to what he can say, in other words—then we need an intermediate step, where the behaviour potential is as it were converted into linguistic potential. This is the concept of what the speaker 'can mean'.

The potential of language is a meaning potential. This meaning potential is the linguistic realization of the behaviour potential; 'can mean' is 'can do' when translated into language. The meaning potential is in turn realized in the language system as lexico-grammatical potential, which is what the speaker 'can say'.

Each stage can be expressed in the form of options. The option in the construction of linguistic forms—sentences, and the like—serve to realize options in meaning, which in turn realize options in behaviour that are interpretable in terms of a social theory.

We can illustrate this point by reference to Basil Bernstein's work in the area of language and social structure (Bernstein, 1967, 1972). On the basis of a theory of social learning, Bernstein identifies a number of social contexts which are crucial to the socialization of the child, for example contexts in which the mother is regulating the child's behaviour or in which she is helping him in learning to carry out some kind of task. These are 'typical contexts of situation', in Firth's sense, but given significance by the theory underlying them.

For any one of these contexts Bernstein is able to specify a range of alternatives that is open to the mother in her interaction with the child. For example, in regulating the child's behaviour she may adopt one (or more) of a number of strategies, which we might characterize in general terms as reasoning, pleading, threatening and the like, but which the theory would suggest represent systematic options in the meanings that are available to her. Bernstein in fact makes use of the term 'meanings' to refer to significant options in the social context; and he regards those as being 'realized' in the behaviour patterns. But this is realization in exactly the linguistic sense, and the behaviour patterns are, at least partly, patterns of meaning in the linguistic sense—the mother's behaviour is largely language behaviour. So the chain of realizations extends from the social theory into the language system.

Hence the behaviour potential associated with the contexts that Bernstein identifies may be expressed linguistically as a meaning potential. Some such step is needed if we are to relate the fundamental concepts of the social theory to recognizable forms and patterns of language behaviour.

A word or two should be said here about the relation of the concept of meaning potential to the Chomskyan notion of competence, even if only very briefly. The two are somewhat different. Meaning potential is defined not in terms of the mind but in terms of the culture; not as what the speaker knows, but as what he can do—in the special sense of what he can do linguistically (what he 'can mean', as we have expressed it). The distinction is important because 'can do' is of the same order of abstraction as 'does'; the two are related simply as potential to actualized potential, and can

44

be used to illuminate each other. But 'knows' is distinct and clearly insulated from 'does'; the relation between the two is complex and oblique, and leads to the quest for a 'theory of performance' to explain the 'does'.

This is related to the question of idealization in linguistics. How does one decide what is systematic and what is irrelevant in language—or, to put the question another way, how does one decide what are different sentences, different phrases and so on, and what are different instances of the same sentence, the same phrase? The issue was raised by Peter Geach in *The State of Language*. His argument is, that in order to understand the logical structure of sentences we have to 'iron out' a lot of the differences that occur in living speech: '. . . idealization which approximates slightly less well to what is actually said, will, by the standards of logical insight into the structures of sentences, pay off better than some analyses that try to come closer to what is actually said' (p. 23).

The philosopher's approach to language is always marked by a very high degree of idealization. In its extreme form, this approach idealizes out *all* natural language as irrelevant and unsystematic and treats only constructed logical languages; a less extreme version is one which accepts sentences of natural language but reduces them all to a 'deep structure' in terms of certain fundamental logical relations. Competence, as defined by Chomsky, involves (as Geach objects) a lower degree of idealization than this. But it is still very high from other points of view, particularly that of anyone interested in language as behaviour. Many behaviourally significant variations in language are simply ironed out, and reduced to the same level as stutterings, false starts, clearings of the throat and the like.

It might be claimed at this point that linguistics is anyway an autonomous science and does not need to look outside itself for criteria of idealization. But this is not a very satisfactory argument. There is a sense in which it is autonomous, and has to be if it is to be relevant to other fields of study: the particulars of language are explained by reference to a general account of language, not by being related piecemeal to social or other non-linguistic phenomena. But this 'autonomy' is conditional and temporary; in the last analysis, we cannot insulate the subject within its own boundaries, and when we come to decide what features in language are to be ignored as unsystematic we are bound to invoke considerations from outside language itself. The problem is met by Chomsky, who regards linguistics as a branch of theoretical psychology. But one may agree with the need for a point of departure from outside language without insisting that this must be sought in one direction and no other—only in psychology, or only in logic. It may just as well be sought in a field such as sociology whose relationship with linguistics has been no less close.

Sociological theory, if it is concerned with the transmission of knowledge or with any linguistically coded type of social act, provides its own criteria for the degree and kind of idealization involved in statements about language; and Bernstein's work is a case in point. In one sense, this is what it is all about. There is always some idealization, where linguistic generalizations are made; but in a sociological context this has to be, on the whole, at a much lower level. We have, in fact, to 'come closer to what is actually said'; partly because the solution to problems may depend on studying what is actually said, but also because even when this is not the case the features that are behaviourally relevant may be just those that the idealizing process most readily irons out. An example of the latter would be features of assertion and doubt, such as *of course*, *I think*, and question tags like *don't they?*, which turn out to be highly significant—not the expressions themselves, but the variations in meaning which they represent, in this case variation in the degree of certainty which the speaker may attach to what he is saying (Turner & Pickvance, 1969).

In order to give an account of language that satisfies the needs of a social theory, we have to be able to accommodate the degree and kind of idealization that is appropriate in that context. This is what the notion of meaning potential attempts to make possible. The meaning potential is the range of *significant* variation that is at the disposal of the speaker. The notion is not unlike Dell Hymes' notion 'communicative competence', except that Hymes defines this in terms of 'competence' in the Chomskyan sense of what the speaker knows, whereas we are talking of a potential—what he can do, in the special linguistic sense of what he can mean—and avoiding the additional complication of a distinction between doing and knowing. This potential can then be represented as systematic options in meaning which may be varied in the degree of their specificity—in what has been called 'delicacy'. That is to say, the range of variation that is being treated as *significant* will itself be variable, with either grosser or finer distinctions being drawn according to the type of problem that is being investigated.

46

3. Language as options

Considering language in its social context, then, we can describe it in broad terms as a behaviour potential; and more specifically as a meaning potential, where meaning is a form of behaving (and the verb *to mean* is a verb of the 'doing' class). This leads to the notion of representing language in the form of options: sets of alternative meanings which collectively account for the total meaning potential.

Each option is available in a stated environment, and this is where Firth's category of system comes in. A system is an abstract representation of a paradigm; and this, as we have noted, can be interpreted as a set of options with an entry condition—a number of possibilities out of which a choice has to be made if the stated conditions of entry to the choice are satisfied. It has the form: if *a*, then either *x* or *y* (or . . .). The key to its importance in the present context is Firth's 'polysystemic principle', whereby (again following this interpretation) the conditions of entry are required to be stated for each set of possibilities. That is to say, for every choice it is to be specified where, under what conditions, that choice is made. The 'where', in Firth's use of the concept of a system, was 'at what point in the structure'; but we interpret it here as 'where in the total network of options'. Each choice takes place in the environment of other choices. This is what makes it possible to vary the 'delicacy' of the description: we can stop wherever the choices are no longer significant for what we are interested in.

The options in a natural language are at various levels: phonological, grammatical (including lexical, which is simply the more specific part within the grammatical) and semantic. Here, where we are concerned with the meaning potential, the options are in the first instance semantic options. These are interpreted as the coding of options in behaviour, so that the semantics is in this sense a behavioural semantics.

The semantic options are in turn coded as options in grammar. Now there are no grammatical categories corresponding exactly to such concepts as those of reasoning, pleading or threatening referred to above. But there may be a prediction, deriving from a social theory, that these will be among the significant behavioural categories represented in the meaning potential. In that case it should be possible to identify certain options in the grammar as being systematic realizations of these categories, since presumably

47

they are to be found somewhere in the language system. We will not expect there to be a complete one-to-one correspondence between the grammatical options and the semantic ones; but this is merely allowing for the normal phenomena of neutralization and diversification that are associated with all stages in the realization chain.

There is nothing new in the notion of associating grammatical categories with higher level categories of a 'socio-' semantic kind. This is quite natural in the case of grammatical forms concerned with the expression of social roles, particularly those systems which reflect the inherent social structure of the speech situation, which cannot be explained in any other way. The principal component of these is the system of mood. If we represent the basic options in the mood system of English in the following way:

$$
\text{independent} \atop \text{clause} \longrightarrow \left[{\text{indicative} \longrightarrow \left[{\text{declarative} \atop \text{interrogative} \longrightarrow \left[{\text{yes/no} \atop \text{``WH-''}} \right.} \right.} \atop \text{imperative} \right.
$$

(to be read 'an independent clause is either indicative or imperative; if indicative, then either declarative or interrogative', and so on), we are systematizing the set of choices whereby the speaker is enabled to assume one of a number of possible communication roles—social roles which exist only in and through language, as functions of the speech situation. The choice of interrogative, for example, means, typically, 'I am acting as questioner (seeker of information), and you are to act as listener and then as answerer (supplier of information)'. By means of this system the speaker takes on himself a role in the speech situation and allocates the complementary role—actually, rather, a particular choice of complementary ones—to the hearer, both while he is speaking and after he has finished.

These 'communication roles' belong to what we were referring to as 'socio-semantics'. They are a special case in that they are a property of the speech situation as such, and do not depend on any kind of a social theory. But the relationship between, say, 'question' in semantics and 'interrogative' in grammar is not really different from that between a behavioural-semantic category such as 'threat' and the categories by which it is realized grammatically. In neither instance is the relationship one-to-one; and while the latter may be rather more complex, a more intensive study of language as social behaviour also suggests a somewhat more complex treatment of traditional notions like those of statement and question. Part of the grammar with which we are familiar is thus a sociological grammar already, although this has usually been confined to a small area where the meanings expressed are 'social' in a rather special sense, that of the social roles created by language itself.

However, the example of the mood system serves to show that, even if we are operating only with the rather oversimplified notions of statement, question, command and the like, categories like these occupy an intermediate level of 'meaning potential' which links behavioural categories to grammatical ones. We do not usually find a significant option in behaviour represented straightforwardly in the grammatical system; it is only in odd instances that what the speaker 'can do' is coded immediately as what he 'can say'. There is a level of what he 'can mean' between the two.

The relation between the levels of meaning and saying, which is one of realization, involves as we have said departures from a regular pattern of one-to-one correspondence. In any particular sociolinguistic investigation, only some of the total possible behavioural options will be under focus of attention; hence we shall be faced especially with instances of 'one-to-many', where one meaning is expressed in different forms. But in such instances we can often invoke the 'good reason' principle, by which one of the possibilities is the 'unmarked' one, that which is chosen to express the meaning in question unless there is good reason to choose otherwise. For example, a question is typically realized in the grammar as an interrogative, and there has to be a 'good reason' for it to be expressed in some other form, such as a declarative. And secondly, the implication of 'one meaning realized by many forms', namely that there is free variation among the possibilities concerned, is unlikely to be the whole truth; it nearly always signifies that there is a more subtle choice in meaning that we have not yet cottoned on to, or that is irrelevant in this particular context.

So a category like that of 'threat', assuming that such a category is identified within the meaning potential, on the basis perhaps of a theory of socialization, will be realized in the language system through a number of different grammatical options. These might include, for example, declarative clauses of a certain type, perhaps first person singular future tense with a verb from a certain lexical set (often identifiable in Roget's *Thesaurus*), and with attached *if* clause, e.g. *if you do that again I'll smack you;* but also certain other forms, negative imperative with *or* (*don't do that again*

49

or . . .), conditioned future attributive clauses with *you* (*you'll be sorry if . . .*), and so on. These may appear at first sight to be merely alternative ways of expressing a threat, in free variation with each other. But it is very likely that on closer inspection they will be found to represent more delicate (though perhaps still significant) options in the meaning potential. At the same time it might be the case that one of them, possibly the first one mentioned above, could be shown on some grounds to be the typical form of threat (perhaps just in this context), the others all being 'marked' variants; we are then committed to stating the conditions under which it is *not* selected but are not required to give any further explanation when it is.

4. An example

Let us consider a hypothetical example of the behaviour potential associated with a particular social context. We will keep within the general framework of Bernstein's theory of socialization, and take up the type of context already mentioned, that of parental control; within this area, we will construct a particular instance that will yield a reasonably simplified illustration. It should be said very clearly that both the pattern of options and the illustrative sentences have been invented for this purpose; they are *not* actual instances from Bernstein's work. But they are modelled closely on Bernstein's work, and draw on many of his underlying concepts. In particular I have drawn on Geoffrey Turner's studies, in which he has made use of the linguistic notion of systems representing options in meaning for the purpose of investigating the role of language in control situations (Turner, 1972).

Let us imagine that the small boy has been playing with the neighbourhood children on a building site. His mother disapproves both of the locale and of the company he has been keeping, and views with particular horror the empty tin or other object he has acquired as a trophy. She wants both to express her disapproval and to prevent the same thing happening again. She might say something like 'that sort of place is not for playing in', or 'I don't like you taking other people's things', or 'they don't want children running about there', or 'just look at the state of your clothes', or 'I'm frightened you'll hurt yourself', or many other things besides.

Various means are open to the mother here for making her intentions explicit. Now, in terms of the actual sentences she might utter, the range of possibilities is pretty well unlimited. But a particular theory about the function of the regulatory context in the socialization of the child would suggest that she is actually operating within a systematic framework of very general options, any one of which (or any one combination) might be expressed through the medium of a wide range of different lexicogrammatical forms. These options represent the meaning potential lying behind the particular instances.

We will assume that the mother is using some form of appeal, as distinct from a direct injunction or a threat. She may simply enunciate a rule, based on her authority as a parent; or she may appeal to reason, and give an explanation of what she wants. Let us call this 'authority or reason'. Secondly, and at the same time, she may formulate her appeal in general or in particular terms, either relating this event to a wider class of situations or treating it on its own; we will say that the appeal may be 'general' or 'particular'. And she may slant her appeal away from the persons involved towards the material environment and the objects in it ('object-oriented'); or she may concentrate on the people ('person-oriented')—in which case the focus of attention may either be on the parent (the mother herself, and perhaps the father as well) or on the child. Finally, if the orientation is towards people, there is another option available, since the appeal may be either 'personal' or 'positional'; that is, relating to the child or herself either as individuals, or in their status in the family, the age group and so on. Thus *you* may mean 'you, Timmy'; or it may mean 'you as my offspring', 'you as a young child' or in some other defined social status.

We may now represent these possibilities in the following way as a network of alternatives:

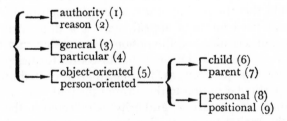

This represents the meaning potential that is open to the mother in the situation, as far as we have taken it in the present discussion.

The categories in this semantic network are not immediately recognizable as linguistic categories. There is no category of 'object-oriented' or 'positional' in the grammar of English, no grammatical system of 'authority/reason'. But if this network of options is a valid account of a part of the range of alternatives that are open to the mother as regards what she 'can mean' in the situation, then the implication is that these options will be found to be realized somewhere in the linguistic system, in the things that she can say.

Any one selection from within this range of options could be realized through a wide range of different grammatical categories and lexical items. Take for example the combination 'authority, general, object-oriented'. The mother might say *that sort of place is not for playing in*, or she might say *we don't go into places like that*, or *other people's things aren't for playing with*, or *we don't take other people's property*; all of these would be instances of the particular combination of options just mentioned. Here we have alternative forms of expression for what are, within the limits of the few distinctions recognized in our illustration, the same selections in meaning. As far as their grammar and vocabulary is concerned, there are certain things common to two or more of these examples which can be related to their common element in their meanings: for example the form . . . *(is/are) not for . . . ing (in/with)*, the form *we don't . . .* , the reference to *place*, and so on. But in other respects they are very different, and involve categories that might not otherwise be brought together from their different places in the description of the grammar, such as *we don't X with/in Y* and *Y is not for X-ing with/in* as forms of disapproval, or the different categories represented by the words *place* and *thing* (including *property*, which can be interpreted as either). Note that *place* and *thing* are grouped together under the option 'object-oriented'; no doubt if the analysis was carried through to a more delicate stage they would then be distinguished, since although both represent non-personalized forms of appeal there is a difference between the notion of territory and the notion of ownership that might be significant. Meanwhile they serve to illustrate a further point, that the analysis seeks to specify as far as possible the contribution made by each particular option to the form of the sentences used. Here, for example, the feature of 'authority' is reflected in the negative and in the modal forms; that of 'general' in the tense and the noun modifiers *that sort of . . . , . . . like that;* that of 'object-oriented' in the words *place*, *thing* and (*other people's*) *property*, coupled with the absence of individualized personal pronouns.

Even though the forms used to express any one meaning selection are very varied, they are nevertheless distinct from those realizing other selections: we must in principle be able to tell what the mother means from what she says, since we are crediting the child with the ability to do so. Here to complete the illustration is a set of possible utterances by the mother representing different selections in the meaning potential. These are not intended to cover the whole of the mother's verbal intervention; some of them would need to be (and all of them could be) accompanied by an explicit injunction such as *you're not to do that again*. They exemplify only options in the type of appeal she is using; as such, each one could occur either alone or in combination with an appeal of one of the other types. The figures following each example indicate, by reference to the network, the options it is assumed to express.

other people's things aren't for playing with (135)
you know you don't play with those sort of boys (1368)
they don't want children running about there (1369)
Daddy doesn't like you to play rough games (1378)
that tin belongs to somebody else (145)
you can go there when you're bigger (1469)
I was worried, I didn't know where you'd got to (1478)
you'll ruin your clothes playing in a place like that (235)
it's not good for you to get too excited (2368)
boys who are well brought up play nice games in the park (2369)
we don't want people to think we don't look after you, do we?
 (2379)
that glass they keep there might get broken (245)
you might have hurt yourself on all that glass (2468)
I'd like you to stay and help me at home (2478)

Not all the possible combinations of options have been exemplified and some of them are unlikely in this particular instance, although probably all could occur. Let us stress again here that both the examples and the network of options, although inspired by Bernstein's work, have been invented for the present discussion, in order to keep the illustration down to a manageable size.

A system network of this kind is open-ended. It may represent only certain very gross distinctions: in the simplest case, just a choice between two possibilities, so that all the meaning potential associated with a particular social context is reduced to 'either this or that'. But it is always capable of accommodating further distinctions—of being made more and more 'delicate'—when these are brought into the picture. Each new distinction that is introduced has implications both 'upwards' and 'downwards':

that is, it is significant as an option in behaviour, and it is systematically (however indirectly) expressed in the language. Only in very restricted types of situation can anywhere near all the linguistic features of an utterance be derived from behaviourally significant options; but then there is no such thing as 'all the linguistic features of an utterance' considered apart from some external criteria of significance. The point is that, as further specification is added to the semantic systems, so more of the linguistic features come to be accounted for. This can be seen in Turner's work, already referred to, in which he is investigating the meaning potential associated with certain contexts of the general kind we have been illustrating.

5. Interpretation of linguistic forms determined by reference to concepts of social theory

In understanding the nature of 'social man', and in particular the processes—and they are largely linguistic processes—whereby the child becomes social man, we are likely to be deeply concerned with those aspects of his experience which centre around social contexts and settings of the kind just exemplified.

We shall not of course expect to assign anything like the whole of an individual's language behaviour to situations of this kind, which can be investigated and interpreted in the light of some significant social theory. The meaning of a poem, or a technical discussion, cannot be expressed in terms of behavioural options. (It can, on the other hand, be related to a set of generalized functions of language which define the total meaning potential of the adult language system; cf. the discussion in the next section.) At the same time, the social contexts and settings for which we can recognize a meaning potential in behavioural terms are not at all marginal or outlandish; and they are contexts which play a significant part in the socialization of the child. The importance of such contexts is given by the social theory from which they are derived.

Not all the distinctions in meaning that may be associated with a context of this kind can be explained by reference to behavioural options which are universally significant in that context. Within the actual words and sentences used there is bound to be much that is particular to the local situation or the shared experience of the individuals concerned. In the illustration given in the last section, the reference to breaking glass or getting hurt by it is obviously
54

specific to a small class of instances of a control situation; and it is likely to be significant only in relation to that setting. It is possible, however, that a highly particular feature of this kind could be the local realization of an option having a general significance: there might be some symbolic value attached to broken glass in the family, having its origin in a particular incident, and we could not know this simply from inspecting the language. And there are general shifted meanings too, extended metaphors whereby, especially in the interaction of adult and child, behavioural options are encoded in highly complex, more or less ritualized linguistic forms; for example the bedtime story, where the princes and the giants and the whole narrative structure collectively express patterns of socialization and interpersonal meanings. Here we are led into the realms of literary interpretation, of levels of meaning in the imaginative mode, of the significance of poetic forms and the like.

Looking to the other end of the scale, we can find settings, for example games, where the language plays an essential part, like pontoon or contract bridge, for which a system of meaning potential will account for a very high proportion of the words and sentences used by the participants (Mohan, 1969). These restricted settings are interesting from the point of view of sociolinguistic method, since they illustrate very well the principle of language as behaviour potential. But they may have little or no significance in themselves as social contexts, relative to any general theory of social behaviour.

What we are referring to as a 'social context' is a generalized type of situation that is itself significant in terms of the categories and concepts of some social theory. The theory may focus attention on different facets of the social structure: not only on forms of socialization and cultural transmission, but also on role relationships, on the power structure and patterns of social control, on symbolic systems, systems of values, of public knowledge and the like. Our example was drawn from the socialization of the child, because that is where most work has been done; but systematic options in language behaviour are not limited to situations of this type. Any situation in which the behavioural options open to the participants are, at least in part, realizations of some general theoretical categories is relevant as a 'social context' in this sense. Hence a particular linguistic feature may have a number of different meanings according to the type of context in which it occurs: for example, *they don't want children in there* might not be any kind of appeal—it might occur in a context that had nothing to do with socialization, not being addressed to a child at all. We could not simply take the linguistic forms for granted, as having just one behavioural interpretation.

More important, perhaps, or at least less obvious, is the fact that even within the same context a linguistic form may have different meanings, since there may be sub-cultural variants in the meaning potential (different 'codes', in Bernstein's sense; cf. Hasan, 1972) typically associated with that context. In other words, assuming that the sentence above was in fact being used in a regulatory context such as the one invented for the illustration, it might still have more than one meaning, given two distinct social groups one of which typically exploited one area of meaning potential (say, 'elaborated code') and the other another ('restricted code'). Within a 'code' in which the typical appeal was positional and non-discretionary, this example would be interpreted as an imperative, whereas in one tending towards more personal and more challengeable appeals it could be taken as a partially explicit rule. The meaning of selecting any one particular feature would be potentially different in the two 'codes', since it would be selected from within a different range of probable alternatives.

We have suggested that this use of a social context corresponds to what Firth meant by the 'typical context of situation', and that it makes the link between the two Malinowskian notions of 'context of situation' and 'context of culture' referred to at the beginning of this paper. It is the social context that defines the limits of the options available; the behavioural alternatives are to this extent context-specific. But the total range of meanings that is embodied in and realized through the language system is determined by the context of culture—in other words by the social structure.

The study of language as social behaviour is in the last resort an account of semantic options deriving from the social structure. Like other hyphenated fields of language study, socio-linguistics reaches beyond the phonological and morphological indices into the more abstract areas of linguistic organization. The concept of socio-linguistics ultimately implies a 'socio-semantics' which is a genuine meeting ground of two ideologies, the social and the linguistic. And this faces both ways. The options in meaning are significant linguistically because selections in grammar and vocabulary can be explained as a realization of them. They are significant sociologically because they provide insight into pat-

56

terns of behaviour that are in turn explainable as realizations of the pragmatic and symbolic acts that are the expressions of the social structure.

In principle we may expect to find some features of the social structure reflected directly in the forms of the language, even in its lower reaches, the morphology and the phonology. The phenomenon of 'accent' is a direct reflection of social structure in the phonetic output. Such low level manifestations may be of little interest, although Labov's (1968) work on the New York dialects showed the potential significance of phonological variables in the social structure of an urban speech community. There is an analogy within the language system itself, where sometimes we find instances of the direct expression of meanings in sounds: voice qualities showing anger, and the like. But in general the forms of expression involve a number of levels of realization—a 'stratal' system (Lamb, 1966)—even within language itself; and this is the more clear when linguistic features are seen as the expression of meanings derived from behaviour patterns outside language: we will not expect to find a direct link between social content and linguistic expression, except in odd cases. The socio-semantics is the pivotal level; it is the interface between the two. Any set of strategies can be represented as a network of options; the point is that by representing it in this way we provide a link in the chain of realizations that relates language to social structure.

6. Importance of socio-linguistic studies for understanding of the nature of language

The investigation of language as social behaviour is not only relevant to the understanding of social structure; it is also relevant to the understanding of language. A network of socio-semantic options—the representation of what we have been calling the 'meaning potential'—has implications in both directions; on the one hand as the realization of patterns of behaviour and, on the other hand, as realized by the patterns of grammar. The concept of meaning potential thus provides a perspective on the nature of language. Language is as it is because of its function in the social structure, and the organization of behavioural meanings should give some insight into its social foundations.

This is the significance of functional theories of language. The essential feature of a functional theory is not that it enables us to enumerate and classify the functions of speech acts, but that it provides a basis for explaining the nature of the language system, since the system itself reflects the functions that it has evolved to serve. The organization of options in the grammar of natural languages seems to rest very clearly on a functional basis, as has emerged from the work of those linguists, particularly of the Prague school, who have been aware that the notion 'functions of language' is not to be equated merely with a theory of language use but expresses the principle behind the organization of the linguistic system.

The options in the grammar of a language derive from and are relatable to three very generalized functions of language which we have referred to as the ideational, the interpersonal and the textual. The specific options in meaning that are characteristic of particular social contexts and settings are expressed through the medium of grammatical and lexical selections that trace back to one or other of these three sources. The status of these terms is that they constitute a hypothesis for explaining what seems to be a fundamental fact about the grammar of languages, namely that it is possible to discern three distinct principles of organization in the structure of grammatical units, as described by Daneš (1964) and others, and that these in turn can be shown to be the structural expression of three rather distinct and independent sets of underlying options.

Those of the first set, the ideational, are concerned with the content of language, its function as a means of the expression of our experience, both of the external world and of the inner world of our own consciousness—together with what is perhaps a separate sub-component expressing certain basic logical relations. The second, the interpersonal, is language as the mediator of role, including all that may be understood by the expression of our own personalities and personal feelings on the one hand, and forms of interaction and social interplay with other participants in the communication situation on the other hand. The third component, the textual, has an enabling function, that of creating text, which is language in operation as distinct from strings of words or isolated sentences and clauses. It is this component that enables the speaker to organize what he is saying in such a way that it makes sense in the context and fulfils its function as a message.

These three functions are the basis of the grammatical system of the adult language. The child begins by acquiring a meaning potential, a small number of distinct meanings that he can express, in two or three functional contexts: he learns to use language for satisfying his material desires ('I want an apple'), for getting others to behave as he wishes ('sing me a song'), and so on. In the first paper, I suggested a list of such contexts for an early stage in his language development. At this stage each utterance tends to have one function only, but as time goes on the typical utterance becomes functionally complex—we learn to combine various uses of language into a single speech act. It is at this point that we need a grammar: a level of organization intermediate between content and expression, which can take the various functionally distinct meaning selections and combine them into integrated structures. The components of the grammatical system are thus themselves functional; but they represent the functions of language in their most generalized form, as these underlie all the more specific contexts of language use.

The meaning potential in any one context is open-ended, in the sense that there is no limit to the distinctions in meaning that we can apprehend. When we talk of what the speaker can do, in this special sense of what he 'can mean', we imply that we can recognize significant differentiations within what he can mean, up to some point or other which will be determined by the requirements of our theory. The importance of a hypothesis about what the speaker can do in a social context is that this makes sense of what he does. If we insist on drawing a boundary between what he does and what he knows, we cannot explain what he does; what he does will appear merely as a random selection from within what he knows. But in the study of language in a social perspective we need both to pay attention to what is said and at the same time to relate it systematically to what might have been said but was not. Hence we do not make a dichotomy between knowing and doing; instead we place 'does' in the environment of 'can do', and treat language as speech potential.

The image of language as having a 'pure' form (*langue*) that becomes contaminated in the process of being translated into speech (*parole*) is of little value in a sociological context. We do not want a boundary between language and speech at all, or between pairs such as langue and parole, or competence and performance— unless these are reduced to mere synonyms of 'can do' and 'does'. A more useful concept is that of a range of behaviour potential determined by the social structure (the context of culture), which is made accessible to study through its association with significant social contexts (generalized contexts of situation), and is actualized by the participants in particular instances of these contexts or situation types.

There is no need to wait until some speaker is observed to produce a particular utterance, before one can take account of the relevant features embodied in it. Socio-linguistic studies are not bounded by the accidental frontiers of the data collected, although they do take such data rather seriously. As Bernstein's work has shown, there are many ways of investigating the language behaviour associated with a social context, ranging from hypothetico-deductive reasoning through various forms of elicitation to hopeful observation. All these are valid parts of the investigator's equipment.

The study of language in a social context tends to involve a rather lower degree of idealization than is customary in a psycho-philosophical orientation, as we have noted already. But there is always some idealization, in any systematic inquiry. It may be at a different place; the type of variation which is least significant for behavioural studies may be just that which is most faithfully preserved in another approach—variation in the ideational meaning, in the 'content' as this is usually understood. We might for example be able to ignore distinctions such as that between singular and plural, or between *cat* and *dog*—if we were using the notion of competence and performance, then these distinctions would be relegated to performance—while insisting on the difference in meaning between *don't do that, you mustn't do that, you're not to do that* and other variants which differ simply in intonation, in pausing and the like.

This overstates the position, no doubt. But it serves to underline the point made earlier: that the object of attention in linguistic studies is not, and never can be, some sort of unprocessed language event. When language is studied in a social perspective, the object of attention is what is usually referred to as 'text', that is, language in a context; and the text, whether in origin it was invented, elicited or recorded, is an idealized construction. But all this means is that a linguistic item—a sentence, or whatever—is well-formed if it is well-formed; there must be criteria from somewhere by which to judge. It is not easy to find these criteria within language; in 'autonomous' linguistics it is in practice usually the orthography that is used to decide what the limits of relevant differentiation are, since the orthography is itself a codified form of idealization (rather as the 'text' of a piece of music is the score). Criteria are found more readily at the interfaces between language

60

and non-language, by reference to something outside language; in a social context, the degree and kind of idealization is determined at the socio-semantic interface. In principle, what is well-formed is whatever can be shown to be interpretable as a possible selection within a set of options based on some motivated hypothesis about language behaviour; and 'motivated' here means extrinsically motivated by reference ultimately to (a theory about) some feature of the social structure.

The perspective is one in which there are two different but related depths of focus. The more immediate aim, from the point of view of linguistics, is the intrinsic one of explaining the nature of language. This implies an 'autonomous' view of linguistics. There is also a further, extrinsic aim, that of explaining features of the social structure, and using language to do so. This implies an 'instrumental' approach. But ultimately the nature of language is explained in terms of its function in the social structure; so the pursuit of the first aim entails the pursuit of the second. To understand language, we examine the way in which the social structure is realized through language: how values are transmitted, roles defined and behaviour patterns made manifest.

The role of language in the educational process is a special aspect of the relation between language and social structure. Bernstein's theories concerning the linguistic basis of educational failure are part of a wider theory of language and society, which encompasses much more than the explanation of the linguistic problems imposed by the educational sysem on the child whose socialization has taken certain forms. Bernstein's concern is with the fundamental problem of persistence and change in the social structure. Language is the principal means of cultural transmission; but if we seek to understand how it functions in this role, it is not enough just to point up odd instances of the reflection of general sociological categories in this or that invented or recorded utterance. An approach to this question presupposes not only a theory of social structure but also a theory of linguistic structure—and hence may lead to further insights into the nature of language, by virtue of the perspective which it imposes. The perspective is a 'socio-semantic' one, where the emphasis is on function rather than on structure; where no distinction is made between language and language behaviour; and where the central notion is something like that of 'meaning potential'—what the speaker 'can mean', with what he 'can say' seen as a realization of it.

Preoccupations of a sociological kind, which as was pointed out

61

at the beginning have for a long time held a place in linguistic studies, assume a greater significance in the light of work such as Bernstein's: not only because Bernstein's social theory is based on a concern with language as the essential factor in cultural transmission, but also because it has far-reaching implications for the nature of language itself. And these, in turn, are very relevant to the educational problems from which Bernstein started. Bernstein has shown the structural relationship between language, the socialization process and education; it is to be expected, therefore, that there will be consequences, for educational theory and practice, deriving from the perspective on language that his work provides. Some concept of the social functioning of language must in any case always underlie the approach of the school towards its responsibility for the pupil's success in his mother tongue.

This paper was first prepared for the Second International Congress of Applied Linguistics, Cambridge, September 1969. A revised version was presented to the Oxford University Linguistic Society, October 1969. It was first printed in *Educational Review*, June 1971.

REFERENCES

Bernstein, B. (1967). 'The Role of Speech in the Development and Transmission of Culture', in Klopf, G. J. and Hohman, W. A. (eds.) *Perspectives on Learning* (Mental Health Materials Center, N.Y.).

Bernstein, B. (1972). 'A Socio-linguistic Approach to Socialization; with some reference to educability', in Gumperz, J. J. and Hymes, D. H. (eds.) *Directions in Sociolinguistics* (Holt, Rinehart & Winston, N.Y.).

Daneš, F. (1964). 'A Three-level Approach to Syntax', *Travaux Linguistiques de Prague*, **1**, 225–240.

Firth, J. R. (1935). 'The Technique of Semantics', *Transactions of the Philological Society*. Reprinted in Firth, J. R. *Papers in Linguistics 1934–1951* (O.U.P., London, 1957).

Firth, J. R. (1968). 'Linguistic Analysis as a Study of Meaning', in Palmer F. R. (ed.) *Selected Papers of J. R. Firth 1952–59* (Longman Linguistics Library, London).

Geach, Peter (1969). 'Should Traditional Grammar be Ended or Mended?—II', in *The State of Language* (*Educational Review*, 22.1, 18–25).

Hasan, Ruqaiya (1971). 'Syntax and semantics', in Morton, J. (ed.) *Biological and Social Factors in Psycholinguistics* (Logos Press, London).

Hasan, Ruqaiya (1972). 'Code, register and social dialect', in Bernstein, B. (ed.) *Class, Codes and Control 2: applied studies towards a sociology of language* (Routledge & Kegan Paul, London).

Hymes, D. H. (in press). 'On Communicative Competence', in Huxley, Renira and Ingram, Elizabeth (eds.), *Mechanisms of Language*

Development (Centre for Advanced Study in the Developmental Sciences, London).

Katz, J. J. and Fodor, J. A. (1963). 'The Structure of a Semantic Theory', *Language*, 39, 170–210.

Labov, W. (1968), 'The Reflection of Social Processes in Linguistic Structures', in Fishman, J. (ed.), *Readings in the Sociology of Language* (Mouton, The Hague).

Lamb, S. M. (1966). *Outline of Stratificational Grammar* (Georgetown U.P., Washington, D.C.).

Malinowski, B. (1923). 'The Problem of Meaning in Primitive Languages', Supplement 1 to Ogden, C. K. and Richards, I. A., *The Meaning of Meaning* (Routledge & Kegan Paul, London).

Malinowski, B. (1935). *Coral Gardens and their Magic*, Volume II (Allen & Unwin, London).

Mohan, B. A. (1969). *An Investigation of the Relationship between Language and Situational Factors in a Card Game, with specific attention to the Language of Instructions*. University of London Ph.D. thesis.

Pike, K. L. (1967). *Language in relation to a Unified Theory of the Structure of Human Behaviour* (2nd revised ed., The Hague, Mouton, Janua Linguarum Series Major 24).

Turner, G. J. (1972). 'Social Class and Children's Language of Control at age 5 and age 7', in Bernstein, B. (ed.) *Class, Codes and Control 2: applied studies towards a sociology of language* (Routledge & Kegan Paul, London).

Turner, G. J. and Pickvance, R. E. (1969). 'Social Class Differences in the Expression of Uncertainty in Five-year-old Children', *Language and Speech*.

Wilkinson, A. (ed.) (1969). *The State of Language* (*Educational Review*, 22.1, University of Birmingham School of Education).

4 Towards a sociological semantics

1. 'Meaning potential' and semantic networks

We shall define language as 'meaning potential': that is, as sets of options, or alternatives, in meaning, that are available to the speaker-hearer.

At each of the levels that make up the linguistic coding system, we can identify sets of options representing what the speaker 'can do' at that level. When we refer to grammar, or to phonology, each of these can be thought of as a range of strategies, with accompanying tactics of structure formation.

There are also sets of options at the two interfaces, the coding levels which relate language to non-language. We use 'semantics' to refer to one of these interfaces, that which represents the coding of the 'input' to the linguistic system. The range of options at the semantic level is the potentiality for encoding in language that which is not language.

The term 'meaning' has traditionally been restricted to the input end of the language system: the 'content plane', in Hjelmslev's terms, and more specifically to the relations of the semantic interface, Hjelmslev's 'content substance'. We will therefore use 'meaning potential' just to refer to the semantic options (although we would regard it as an adequate designation for language as a whole).

Semantics, then, is 'what the speaker can mean'. It is the strategy that is available for entering the language system. It is one form of, or rather one form of the realization of, behaviour potential; 'can mean' is one form of 'can do'. The behaviour potential may be realized not only by language but also by other means. Behavioural strategies are outside language but may be actualized through the medium of the language system.

64

Let us take as an example the use of language by a mother for the purpose of controlling the behaviour of a child. This example is invented, but it is based on actual investigations of social learning—including, among a number of different contexts, that of the regulation of children's behaviour by the mother—carried out in London under the direction of Professor Basil Bernstein. In particular I have drawn on the work of Geoffrey Turner, who has undertaken much of the linguistic analysis of Professor Bernstein's material and shown how the networks of semantic options can serve as a bridge between the sociological and the purely linguistic conceptual frameworks (see reference in Paper 3).

The small boy has been playing with the neighbourhood children on a building site, and has come home grasping some object which he has acquired in the process. His mother disapproves, and wishes both to express her disapproval and to prevent him doing the same thing again. She has a range of alternatives open to her, some of which are non-linguistic: she can smack him. But supposing she elects to adopt linguistic measures, the sort of thing she might say would be:

(1) that's very naughty of you
(2) I'll smack you if you do that again
(3) I don't like you to do that
(4) that thing doesn't belong to you
(5) Daddy would be very cross

These represent different means of control, which might be characterized as (1) categorization of behaviour in terms of disapproval or approval on moral grounds; (2) threat of punishment linked to repetition of behaviour; (3) emotional appeal; (4) categorization of objects in terms of social institution of ownership; (5) warning of disapproval by other parent. And we could add others, e.g. (6) *you're making Mummy very unhappy by disobeying* (control through emotional blackmail), (7) *that's not allowed* (control through categorization of behaviour in terms of operation of rule), etc.

The mother's behaviour could also be described linguistically, in terms of grammatical systems of mood, transitivity and so on. For example, (1) is a relational clause of the attributive (ascription) type where the child's act is referred to situationally as *that* and has ascribed to it, in simple past tense, an attribute expressed by an attitudinal adjective *naughty*, the attribution being explicitly tied to the child himself by the presence of the qualifier *of you*.

65

In (2) we have a hypotactic clause complex in which the main clause is a transitive clause of action in simple future tense with *smack* as process, *I* as actor and *you* as goal, the dependent clause being a conditional, likewise of the action type, with situationally-referring process *do that* and actor *you*.

But these two accounts of the mother's behaviour, the sociological and the linguistic, are unrelated, except in that they are descriptions of the same phenomena. In order to try and relate them, let us describe the mother's verbal behaviour in the form of a system of semantic options, options which we can then relate to the social situation on the one hand and to the grammatical systems of the language on the other.

Figure 1 is a first attempt at a semantic network for this context. It uses a simultaneous characterization of the options in terms of two variables: (i) the type of control adopted and (ii) the orientation of the control. System (ii) is redundant for the purpose of discriminating among the present examples, since all are uniquely specified in system (i); but it adds a generalization, suggesting other combinations of options to be investigated, and it specifies other features which we might be able to link up with particular features in the grammar.

2. Provisional version of a semantic network

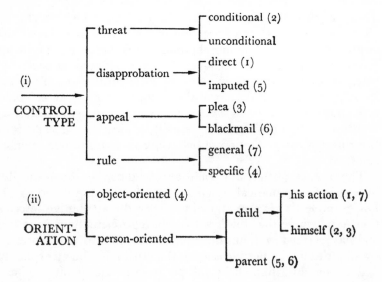

This is the simplest form of such a network, specifying merely options and sub-options. It reads: 'select threat *or* disapprobation *or* appeal *or* rule; *and either* object-oriented *or* person-oriented. *If* threat, *then either* conditional *or* unconditional,' and so on. Numbers in parentheses indicate how these options relate to the examples that were given above.

Now there is probably no category of 'threat' or 'blackmail' or 'object-oriented' to be found in the grammar of English. These are semantic not grammatical categories. But it may be possible to specify what are the grammatical realizations of semantic categories of this kind. For instance, 'threat' is likely to be realized as a transitive clause of action with *you* as Goal, and with a verb of a particular sub-class as Process, in simple future tense. The combination of 'disapprobation' and 'person-oriented : action' leads us to predict an attributive clause type, in which the action that is being censured is expressed as the 'attribuend' (the Goal of the attribution) and the Attribute is some adjective of the attitudinal class. Thus the semantic options are relatable to recognizable features in the grammar, even though the relationship will often be a rather complex one.

A semantic option may, in addition, have more than one possible realization in the grammar. For instance, 'threat' might be realized as a modalized action clause with *you* as Actor, e.g. *you'll have to stay indoors if you do that*. Where there are such alternatives, these are likely in the end to turn out to represent more delicate semantic options, systematic sub-categories rather than free variants (see Section 6 below). But until such time as a distinction in meaning (i.e. in their function in realizing higher-level options) is found, they can be treated as instances of diversification. This is the same phenomenon of diversification as is found in the relations between other pairs of strata.

We have not expressed, in the network, everything that was included in the description of the forms of control; there is no reference yet to the category of 'ownership', or to the fact that the disapproval is 'moral' disapproval. It is not yet clear what these contrast with; they might be fully determined by some existing option. But they are expressed in the same way, by realization in linguistic forms, and there is no difficulty in adding them as semantic options once their value in the meaning potential can be established.

3. The semantic network as a statement of potential at that stratum

A network such as that in the previous section is a specification of meaning potential. It shows, in this instance, what the mother is doing when she regulates the behaviour of the child. Or rather, it shows what she CAN do: it states the possibilities that are open to her, in the specific context of a control situation. It also expresses the fact that these are LINGUISTIC possibilities; they are options in meaning, realized in the form of grammatical, including lexical, selections.

These networks represent paradigmatic relations on the semantic stratum (assuming a tri-stratal model of the linguistic system, with semantic, lexicogrammatical and phonological levels); so we shall refer to them as 'semantic networks'. A semantic network is a hypothesis about patterns of meaning, and in order to be valid it must satisfy three requirements. It has to account for the range of alternatives at the semantic stratum itself; and it has to relate these both 'upwards', in this instance to categories of some general social theory or theory of behaviour, and 'downwards', to the categories of linguistic form at the stratum of grammar.

In the first place, therefore, we are making a hypothesis about what the speaker can do, linguistically, in a given context: about what meanings are accessible to him. In order to do this we need not only to state the options that are available but, equally, to show how they are systematically related to one another. As has been pointed out earlier, this is the purpose of the system network. It is a general statement of the paradigmatic relations at the stratum in question, and therefore it constitutes, at one and the same time, a description of each meaning selection and an account of its relationship to all the others—to all its 'agnates', in Gleason's formulation.

From the network we can derive a paradigm of all the meaning selections. This is the set of 'well-formed selection expressions' from the network in question, and the network asserts that these and no others are possible.

The network is however open-ended in delicacy. We take as the starting point the total set of possible meaning selections, and proceed by progressive differentiation on the basis of systematic contrasts in meaning. It is always possible to add further specification; but it is never necessary to do so, so we can stop at the point where any further move in delicacy is of no interest. For instance, if for the purposes of a particular investigation the social theory places no value on the distinction between different types of 'appeal' in a control situation, there is no need to incorporate any sub-systems of 'appeal' into the semantic network.

We use the paradigm to test predictions about meaning selections that might be expected to occur. This can be illustrated from the same general context, that of parental regulation of child behaviour; but we will use a modified form of the network so that the illustration is kept down to a manageable size. Let us postulate the following network of options:

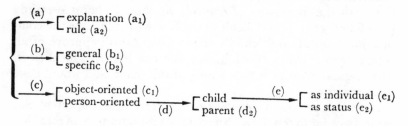

This specifies that the following meaning selections occur:

$(a_1\ b_1\ c_1)$	$(a_1\ b_2\ c_1)$	$(a_2\ b_1\ c_1)$	$(a_2\ b_2\ c_1)$
$(a_1\ b_1\ d_2)$	$(a_1\ b_2\ d_2)$	$(a_2\ b_1\ d_2)$	$(a_2\ b_2\ d_2)$
$(a_1\ b_1\ e_1)$	$(a_1\ b_2\ e_1)$	$(a_2\ b_1\ e_1)$	$(a_2\ b_2\ e_1)$
$(a_1\ b_1\ e_2)$	$(a_1\ b_2\ e_2)$	$(a_2\ b_1\ e_2)$	$(a_2\ b_2\ e_2)$

We can construct a set of possible exponents, one for each:

$(a_1\ b_1\ c_1)$ playing in that sort of place ruins your clothes
$(a_1\ b_1\ d_2)$ grown-ups like to be tidy
$(a_1\ b_1\ e_1)$ it's not good for you to get too excited
$(a_1\ b_1\ e_2)$ boys who are well brought up play nice games in the park
$(a_1\ b_2\ c_1)$ all that glass might get broken
$(a_1\ b_2\ d_2)$ Daddy doesn't like you to play rough games
$(a_1\ b_2\ e_1)$ you might hurt yourself
$(a_1\ b_2\ e_2)$ you ought to show Johnny how to be a good boy
$(a_2\ b_1\ c_1)$ other people's things aren't for playing with
$(a_2\ b_1\ d_2)$ Mummy knows best
$(a_2\ b_1\ e_1)$ you mustn't play with those kind of boys
$(a_2\ b_1\ e_2)$ little boys should do as they're told
$(a_2\ b_2\ c_1)$ that tin belongs to somebody else
$(a_2\ b_2\ d_2)$ I told you I didn't want you to do that

(a₂ b₂ e₁)   you'll get smacked next time
(a₂ b₂ e₂)   you can go there when you're bigger

The paradigm seems to be valid. We have substituted just two types of control, 'by rule' and 'by explanation', each of which may be general or specific; and we have sub-divided 'child-oriented' into the more significant system of 'child as individual' versus 'child as status'.

As an example of a wrong prediction, if we kept the original network, which had 'child-oriented : child's action' versus 'child-oriented: child himself', and showed this system in free combination with the four types of control, we should almost certainly have found gaps. It is difficult to see how we could have the combination 'appeal' and 'child's action'; one can disapprove of an action, or give rules about it, but one can hardly appeal to it. The original network is thus wrong at this point, and would have to be rewritten.

Here is a rewritten version of it, corrected in respect of this error. In order to test it, we can write out the paradigm of meaning selections and, for each one, construct an example which would be acceptable as an exponent of it.

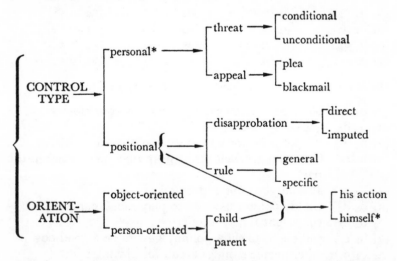

Here we have introduced two further conventions. The option '*either* child's action *or* child himself' depends on the selection of *both* 'control type : positional' *and* 'orientation : child'; there is an intersection at this point in the network. Secondly, this system is characterized by the presence of an unmarked term, 'child him-

70

self', indicated by the asterisk. An unmarked option is always unmarked 'with respect to' some other option, here that of 'positional', also marked with an asterisk. The meaning is: 'if the speaker selects the "personal" control type, then if the orientation is to the child it must always be to the "child himself"'. The unmarked option is that which must be selected if one part of the entry condition is not satisfied, some other feature being selected which then determines the choice.

4. The semantic network as realization of behaviour patterns

In the second place, as is shown by what was said above, the semantic network is an account of how social meanings are expressed in language. It is the linguistic realization of patterns of behaviour.

We have stressed at various points that a linguistic description is a statement of what the speaker can mean; and that 'meaning', in its most general sense, includes both function within one level and realization of elements of a higher level. These 'higher level' elements will, at one point, lie outside the confines of what we recognize as language.

In the sociological context, the relevant extra-linguistic elements are the behaviour patterns that find expression in language. It is convenient to treat these under two headings: social, and situational.

First, there are the specifically social aspects of language use: the establishment and maintenance of the individual's social roles, the establishment of familiarity and distance, various forms of boundary maintenance, types of personal interaction and so on. These are largely independent of setting, but relate to generalized social contexts, such as those of mother and child already referred to.

The social contexts themselves are in turn dependent for their identification on a social theory of some kind, for instance Bernstein's theories of socialization and social learning. From such a theory, we are able to establish which contexts are relevant to the study of particular problems. The behavioural options are specific to the given social context, which determines their meaning; for example, 'threat' in a mother–child control context has a different significance from 'threat' in another social context, such as the operation of a gang. This may affect its realization in language.

71

Secondly, there are the situation types, the settings, in which language is used. These enable us to speak of 'text', which may be defined as 'language in setting'. Here we are concerned not with behaviour patterns that are socially significant in themselves but with socially identifiable units—transactions of various kinds, tasks, games, discussions and the like—within which the behaviour is more or less structured. Mitchell's classic study 'The language of buying and selling in Cyrenaica' provides an instance of a well-defined setting. The structure, in fact, may lie wholly within the text, as typically it does in a work of literature, or an abstract discussion; from the sociological point of view, these situation-independent uses of language are the limiting case, since the 'setting' is established within and through the language itself.

The behaviour patterns that we derive from social contexts and settings are thus intrinsic to sociological theory; they are arrived at in the search for explanations of social phenomena, and are independent of whatever linguistic patterns may be used to express them. The function of the semantic network is to show how these 'social meanings' are organized into linguistic meanings, which are then realized through the different strata of the language system. But whereas the social meanings, or behaviour patterns, are specific to their contexts and settings, their linguistic reflexes are very general categories such as those of transitivity, of mood and modality, of time and place, of information structure and the like. The input to the semantic networks is sociological and specific; their output is linguistic and general. The rationale for this is discussed in Section 6 below.

This means that in sociological linguistics the criteria for selecting the areas of study are sociological. We investigate those contexts and settings that are socially significant, for instance those concerned with the transmission of cultural values. At the same time, it is not irrelevant that language has evolved in the service of social functions, so we may expect to take account of social factors in explaining the nature of language. There is therefore a clear LINGUISTIC motivation for studies of a socio-linguistic kind.

Here is an example drawn from a clearly-defined setting the game of pontoon (vingt-et-un). This is a social context with closely circumscribed behaviour patterns, namely the rules of the game. These define what the participant can do. The semantic network does not describe the rules of the game; it specifies what are the verbalized options in play—what the participant 'can mean', in our terms.

The form of play has been described by Bernard Mohan in a flow-chart (see the reference in Paper 3). Here is a semantic network showing the meaning potential for one move, by a player other than the banker:

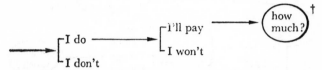

Now, having requested one card the player has the option of requesting another. Is this an option in meaning, or merely a rule of the game? If we reorganize it as part of the meaning potential, there is a recursive option in the semantic network (Figure 5):

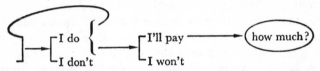

We might even think of extending this into the grammar: an example such as *buy for two, buy for two, twist, stick* would then form a single paratactic univariate structure. This would be somewhat uneconomical, though as a matter of fact there is some evidence in its favour. It would be uneconomical because we should have to build in to the grammar a number of special features associated with it: the absence of *and*, the possibility of interruption, and so on. The evidence for it is that the player does normally use the intonation pattern appropriate to co-ordination, e.g.

//3 buy for / *two* //3 buy for / *two* //3 *twist* //1 *stick* // with the (normally non-final) tone 3 representing the HOPE that he will be able to request another card. The fact that the entire structure is not planned at the start is immaterial; this may be a general characteristic of univariate structures. It is interesting that in contract bridge many players use this 'non-final' intonation when bidding as a means of inviting their partner to make a higher bid. They distinguish

//3 three / *clubs* // 'I want you to raise it' from
//1 three / *clubs* // 'and don't you go any higher!'.

† 'I do' = 'I request another card'
  'I don't' = 'I do not want another card' realized as *stick*!
  'I'll pay' = 'I will pay for the card' realized as *buy for* . . .!
  'I won't' = 'I will not pay for the card' realized as *twist*!
  'how much?' = 'I will pay the sum specified' realized as [numeral following *buy for*]

73

If we do recognize a recursive option in the semantics, we must also take account of the fact that the player has first to pass through the option 'I can/cannot request another card', as follows:

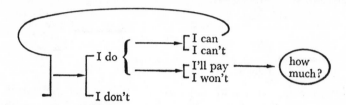

We add to this the condition that if on the third time round he still selects 'I can' he must nevertheless proceed to 'I don't', which is realized this time as *five and under*.

Here, then, there is some indeterminacy between the strata. Whether in fact we represented the whole of one 'turn' in the semantic network would probably depend on the nature of the problem being investigated. But it is possible to do so, since the system can be reduced to a single complex expression of request.

It is, of course, the fall of the cards that determines whether the player has the RIGHT to request another card or not. But the conditions under which he may or may not do so are part of the rules of the game; they belong to a higher-stratum context. The semantics cannot specify what are the rules of the game.

Likewise we could make a flow-chart for another game setting, one that is reasonably closed (e.g. the bidding system of contract bridge), and construct an associated semantic network. For this it would be necessary to identify some unit that is appropriate as the domain of the semantic options. For pontoon, we suggested one 'turn'; here it would probably be one bid. The semantics then specifies what is the set of possible bids. It does not specify the circumstances in which the player has the right to make a particular bid—still less those in which it would be a good one!

To summarize: Grammar is what the speaker CAN SAY, and is the realization of what he MEANS. Semantics is what he CAN MEAN; and we are looking at this as the realization of what he DOES. But it is 'realization' in a somewhat different sense, because what he CAN DO lies outside language (and therefore, as we expressed it above, semantics cannot tell us the rules of the game). Some of the behaviour potential, the 'can do', can be expressed in sociological terms; not all, since not all language behaviour has its setting in identifiable social contexts, and much of that which has is not

74

explainable by reference to the setting. In sociological linguistics we are interested in that part of language behaviour which CAN be related to social factors and stated in these terms. We examine areas which are relatively circumscribed; and we select those which are of intrinsic interest—noting at the same time, however, that the investigation of the socio-linguistic interface may also shed valuable light on the nature of language itself.

5. The semantic network as realized in the grammatical system

In the third place, the semantic network is the 'input' to the grammar. The semantic network forms the bridge between behaviour patterns and linguistic forms.

We cannot, as a rule, relate behavioural options directly to the grammar. The relationship is too complex, and some intermediate level of representation is needed through which we express the meaning potential that is associated with the particular behavioural context. It is this intermediate level that constitutes our 'sociological' semantics. The semantic network then takes us, by a second step, into the linguistic patterns that can be recognized and stated in grammatical terms.

In some instances, the semantic network leads directly to the 'formal items'—to the actual words, phrases and clauses of the language. This is likely to happen only where there is a closed set of options in a clearly circumscribed social context.

Systems of greetings would often be of this kind. Here is a semantic network for a greeting system in middle-class British English:

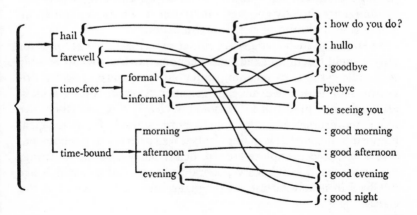

On the right are the items realizing the meaning selections; the colon is used *ad hoc* to show that these are on a different stratum.

[This display leaves out a number of facts, treating them by implication as behavioural (as 'rules of the game') and not semantic. There are severe limitations on the use of time-bound forms, other than *good night*, as valedictions; they are used mainly in the conclusion of trading transactions, and are probably disappearing. The form *how do you do?* is used only in the context of a new acquaintance, a time-bound form being required in the formal greeting of old acquaintances. Such factors could be incorporated into the network, if they are regarded as part of the 'meaning potential'; but for the present discussion it does not matter whether they are or not.]

In this instance, we can go straight from the options to the actual phrases by which they are realized, the 'formal items' as we have termed them. There is no need for any intervening level of grammatical systems and structures.

A number of more specific social contexts, and recurrent situation types, are likely to have this property, that the formal items, the words and phrases used, are directly relatable to the options in the semantic network. Apart from games, and greetings systems, which have already been exemplified, other instances would include musical terms (*adagio*, etc.), instructions to telephone operators, and various closed transactions such as buying a train or bus ticket. If we ignore the fact that the formal items are in turn re-encoded, or realized, as phonological items ('expressions'), which are in turn put out as speech (or the equivalent in the written medium), these are rather like non-linguistic semiotic systems, such as those of traffic signs and care labels on clothing, where the meanings are directly encoded into patterns in the visual medium. There is a minimum of stratal organization.

In language such systems are rather marginal; they account for only a small fraction of the total phenomena. In order to be able to handle systems of meaning potential which are of wider linguistic significance we have to consider types of setting which, although they may still be reasonably clearly circumscribed, are much more open and also much more general. In sociological linguistics the interest is in linguistic as well as in social phenomena, and so we need to explore areas of behaviour where the meanings are expressed through very general features, features which are involved in nearly all uses of language, such as transitivity in the clause.

In other words, for linguistic as well as for sociological reasons we should like to be able to account for grammatical phenomena by reference to social contexts whenever we can, in order to throw some light on why the grammar of languages is as it is. The more we are able to relate the options in grammatical systems to meaning potential in the social contexts and behavioural settings, the more insight we shall gain into the nature of the language system, since it is in the service of such contexts and settings that language has evolved.

This is no more than to recognize that there is a 'stratal' relation of the usual kind between grammar and semantics. In general the options in a semantic network will be realized by selections of features in the grammar—rather than 'bypassing' the grammatical systems and finding direct expression as formal items.

We have exemplified this already in discussing the realization of semantic categories such as that of 'threat'. Let us return to this instance, and add further examples. The following are some possible expressions of 'threat' and of 'warning' as semantic options in a regulatory context:

I'll smack you
Daddy'll smack you
you'll get smacked
I'll smack you
Daddy'll smack you } { if you do that again
you'll get smacked } { if you go on doing that
you do that again } and } { I'll smack you
you go on doing that } } { Daddy'll smack you
don't you do that again } or } { you'll get smacked
you stop doing that }
I shall be cross with you
Daddy'll be cross with you
you'll fall down
you'll get hurt; you'll hurt yourself
you'll get dirty
you'll cut your hands; your hands'll get cut
you'll tear your clothes; your clothes'll get torn
your feet'll get wet
you'll get yourself hurt
you'll get your hands cut
you'll get your feet wet

We suggested earlier, as a generalization, that 'threat' could be realized by an action clause in simple future tense, having *you* either as Goal, or as Actor together with a modulation. We can now take this a little further, building up the network as we go.

The 'threat' may be a threat of physical punishment. Here the clause is of the action type, and, within this, of intentional or voluntary action, not supervention (i.e. the verb is of the *do* type, not the *happen* type). The process is a two-participant process, with the verb from a lexical set expressing 'punishment by physical violence', roughly that of § 972 (PUNISHMENT) in Roget's *Thesaurus*, or perhaps the intersection of this with § 276 (IMPULSE). The tense is simple future. The Goal, as already noted, is *you*; and the clause may be either active, in which case the agency of the punishment is likely to be the speaker (*I* as Actor), or passive, which has the purpose of leaving the agency unspecified. It is not entirely clear whether, if the Actor is other than *I*, the utterance is a threat or a warning; but it seems likely that in *Daddy'll smack you* the speaker is committing another person to a course of action on her behalf, so we still treat it as 'threat':

Any one of these threats may then be accompanied by a condition referring to the repetition or continuation by the child of whatever he was doing, and here we can specify almost the entire form of the clause: action verb substitute *do that*, Actor *you*,

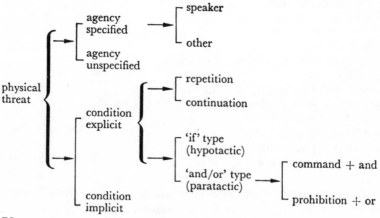

Conjunction *if*, and either auxiliary of aspect (*go on*) or aspectual adverb (*again*).

Probably all threats are conditional in this context, so the choice is between a condition that is explicit and one that is implicit. Note the alternative form of the condition—as an imperative clause (which must come first) in a paratactic: co-ordinate structure, either command with 'and' or prohibition with 'or'. (The prohibition also occurs by itself as a form of regulatory behaviour, e.g. *don't you do that again!*; but that is left out because it is not a threat.)

There are two other sub-categories of 'threat' among the examples given. One has a relational clause of the attributive type, having as Attribute an adjective expressive of anger or displeasure (Roget § 900 RESENTMENT) and *I* or a committed other person as Attribuend. The other is an action clause with the action modulated by necessity (e.g. *must, have to*), *you* as Actor and a wide range of punitive states of which little more can be specified. Contextually the former constitutes a threat of mental punishment, the latter a threat of restraint on the child's own behavioural options:

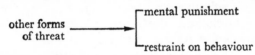

Next, there is the distinct category of 'warning'. This also is inherently conditional; we have given only examples without conditions but all could occur in an explicitly conditional form.

The warning specifies something that will happen to the child—something considered to be undesirable—if he does whatever it is he is being told not to do. The warning may relate to some process in which the child will become involved. Here the clause is of the 'action' type; it is, however, always 'superventive'—the child is involved against his own volition. The action in question may be one that is inherently unintentional, represented by a verb of the 'happen' type; in this case the meaning is 'do involuntarily' and the voice is active (e.g. *fall down*). Otherwise, if the action is inherently intentional, with a verb of the 'do' type (typically from a sub-set of Roget § 659 DETERIORATION, or § 688 FATIGUE), the meaning is 'have done to one, come in for' and the voice is non-active: either passive: mutative (e.g. *get hurt*) or reflexive (*hurt yourself*), according to whether or not some unspecified agency is implied that is external to the child himself.

Alternatively, the warning may specify an attribute that the

79

child will acquire. Here the clause is relational: attributive, also in the mutative form (i.e. *get* rather than *be*), and the attribute is an adjective of undesirable physical condition such as *wet, sore, tired, dirty* (in Roget § 653 UNCLEANNESS, § 655 DISEASE, § 688 or elsewhere).

In all these clauses, there is only one participant, and it is always *you*. This may be Actor, Goal or Attribuend; but it always has the generalized function of Affected (K in Paper 2, Figure 4).

So far it has been assumed that the warning relates to the child himself. But it may relate instead to a part of his body or an item of his clothing (e.g. *you'll cut your hands, your clothes'll get muddy*). And finally the consequence has been represented as something that will happen to the child (or, again, to his person) without any specified agency: *you'll fall down, you'll get dirty, you'll get hurt, you'll hurt yourself, you'll cut your hands, you'll tear your clothes.* (Note that the last two are still superventive; *you'll tear your clothes* means 'your clothes will get torn', not 'you will tear your clothes deliberately'; cf. *you'll hurt yourself.*) But it may be represented instead as something which he will bring upon himself. In this case, the clause has the resultative form *you'll get your . . . (self,* part of the body or item of clothing) *hurt, dirty, torn* etc.; here *yourself, your clothes* etc. function as Affected and *you* as Agent.

Here is the network of warnings at this point:

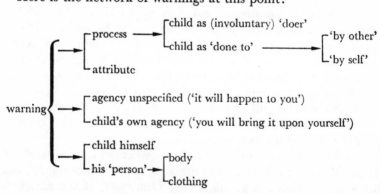

In this network we have shown the three options 'process, or attribute; agency unspecified, or child's own agency; the child himself, or his person' as being independent variables. This asserts that all logically possible combinations can occur, including those formed with the sub-options dependent on 'process' and on 'his person'; there is a total paradigm of $4 \times 2 \times 3 = 24$ meaning selections. But only some of these are given in the examples, and this illustrates once again the point made earlier, that the paradigm defined by a system network provides a means of testing for all possibilities. If, when the paradigm is written out, it is found that not all combinations can occur, the network needs to be amended.

Here it will be found that the primary options are in fact independent. But the sub-option of 'child as doer, or child as done to', dependent on the selection of 'process', turns out to be at least partly determined in all environments except one, that of 'agency unspecified AND child himself'. In the environment of 'child's own agency' it is fully determined—naturally: since the child is represented as bringing the consequence on himself, there is no distinction of how the process comes about. In the remaining environment, that of 'agency unspecified AND child's person', it is partly determined: the opposition 'child as doer, or child as done to' is still valid, but the reflexive does not occur. This again is to be expected, since it is not the child himself but his person that is involved.

The final version of the network, showing both threat and warning, is therefore as follows:

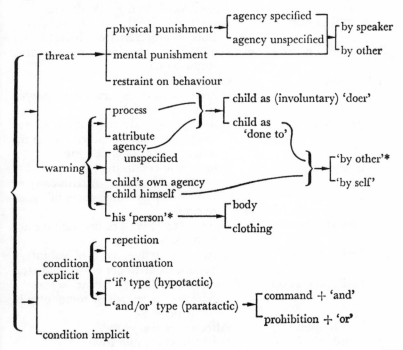

81

6. Semantic networks and grammar

In the last section we have been looking at the semantic network from the point of view of its relation 'downwards', seeing how we get from it into the grammar. In particular, we were considering the question to what extent the grammatical and lexical properties of the sentences used by the speaker in the speech situation—in our example, the mother regulating the behaviour of her child—can be 'predicted' from a semantics of behaviour, a semantics based on social context and setting.

Let us make this a little more specific by writing out the realization statements associated with the features in the network of threats and warnings:

1	threat	clause: declarative
2	physical punishment	clause: action: voluntary (*do* type); effective (two-participant): Goal = *you*; future tense; positive; verb from Roget § 972 (or 972, 276)
3	agency specified	voice: active
4	agency unspecified	voice: passive
5	by speaker	Actor/Attribuend = *I*
6	by other	Actor/Attribuend = *Daddy*, etc.
7	mental punishment	clause: relational: attributive: Attribute = adjective from Roget § 900
8	restraint on behaviour	clause: action; modulation: necessity; Actor = *you*
9	warning	clause: declarative
10	process	clause: action: superventive (*happen* type)
11	attribute	clause: relational: attributive: mutative; Attribute = adjective from Roget § 653, 655, 688 etc.
12	agency unspecified	clause: non-resultative; Affected (Actor, Goal or Attribuend) = *you/yourself* or some form of 'your person'
13	child as 'doer'	voice: active; verb of involuntary action; Actor = *you*
14	child as 'done to'	voice: non-active; verb of voluntary action, from Roget § 659, 688 etc.
15	child's own agency	clause: resultative; Agent = *you*; Affected = *yourself* or some form of 'your person'
16	child himself	Affected = *you/yourself*
17	by 'other'	voice: passive: mutative

18 by 'self'	voice: reflexive
19 his 'person'	Affected: some form of 'your person'
20 body	'your person' $= your +$ part of body
21 clothing	'your person' $= your +$ item of clothing
22 condition explicit	clause complex; clause (1 or β): action: effective; anaphoric: verb substitute $= do\ that;$ Actor $= you$
23 repetition	aspect: *again*
24 continuation	aspect: *go on/stop* (in negative) . . . *ing*
25 'if' type	clause complex: hypotactic: clause β conditional: *if*
26 'and/or' type	clause complex: paratactic: clause 1 imperative
27 command + 'and'	clause 1 positive; *and*
28 prohibition + 'or'	clause 1 negative (including form with *stop*); *or*
29 condition implicit	(——)

Two points suggest themselves immediately. The first is that in this particular example we have been able to generate a great deal of the grammar in this way. We have given some specification of many of the principal grammatical features of the clause or clause complex: paratactic complex with *and* or *or*, hypotactic complex with *if*, or simple clause; the clause type in respect of transitivity (action clause, relational clause etc.); whether positive or negative, in some cases; and something of the selection in mood and in modality and tense. We have also determined the items occupying some of the participant functions, especially the pronouns *I* and *you*. We have not been able to specify the exact lexical items, but we have been able to narrow down many of them fairly closely by using the notion of a lexical set as exemplified in Roget's *Theasaurus*. A significant portion of the clause, in this instance, can be related to its 'meaning' in terms of some higher level of a socio-behavioural kind.

Secondly, the features that we have been able to specify are not marginal areas of the grammar but are categories of the most general kind, such as mood and transitivity. Nearly every clause in English makes some selection in these systems, and in this instance we were able to relate the choice to the social function of the utterance. For example in the 'warning' network, where the mother makes explicit the nature of the consequence that will follow if the child continues or repeats the undesired behaviour, we were able to get to the core of the English transitivity system, and to see what lay behind the choice of active or passive or reflexive verb forms. We did not go very far in delicacy, and certainly there would be limits on how far we could go; but we did not reach those limits in this example, and in a more detailed study it would be possible both to extend and to elaborate the semantic network.

It must be made clear, however, that the example chosen was a favourable instance. We would not be able to construct a socio-semantic network for highly intellectual abstract discourse, and in general the more self-sufficient the language (the more it creates its own setting, as we expressed it earlier) the less we should be able to say about it in these broadly sociological, or social, terms. Of the total amount of speech by educated adults in a complex society, only a small proportion would be accessible to this approach. Against this, however, we may set the fact that the instances about which we *can* say something, besides being favourable, are also interesting and significant in themselves, because they play a great part, almost certainly the major part, in the child's early language learning experience. They are in fact precisely those settings from which he learns his language, because both language and setting are accessible to his observation. He can see what language is being used for, what the particular words and structures are being made to achieve, and in this way he builds up his own functionally-based language system. So even if with some adults the types of social context that are most favourable for socio-linguistic investigation become as it were 'minority time' usages, this does not mean they are unimportant to the understanding of the language system.

*   *   *

We need to say a little more here about the relation between the semantics and the grammar, or level of linguistic form. We began with an example of the simplest type of relation, one of 'bypassing', where the semantic options could be as it were wired directly into a small set of words and phrases, without our having to take account of any intervening organization. This situation does arise, but only rather marginally. In the more usual and more significant instances we have to go through a level of grammatical organization, in order to show how the semantic options are put into effect. This in fact is the definition of grammar—the term 'grammar' being used, as always, for the level of linguistic form,

84

including both grammatical (in the sense of syntax and morphology) and lexical features. Grammar is the level at which the various strands of meaning potential are woven into a fabric; or, to express this non-metaphorically, the level at which the different meaning selections are integrated so as to form structures.

We also express the grammar in networks, such as those of transitivity, mood and modality. The question is, then: what is the relation between the networks of the grammar and the semantic networks that we have been illustrating here?

We already have the notion of 'pre-selection' between networks, in relating grammar and phonology. For instance, in the phonology of English there is a system of tone, which we show as a network at the phonological stratum. But the selection in this system is fully determined by the grammar: there is 'pre-selection' of the phonological options. The pattern is rather complex, because there is no one-to-one correspondence between options in the grammar and options in the phonology; a large number of different grammatical systems are realized by means of selection in the phonological system of tone. But it is not impossible to find them out.

Between semantic and grammatical networks the same relation obtains. The grammatical options are the realizations of the semantic ones. Again, there is no one-to-one correspondence: there is what Lamb calls 'interlocking diversification' (many-to-many). But, again, the relations can be stated: the selection of a given option in the semantic network is realized by some selection in the networks of the grammar. Very often more than one grammatical feature has to be pre-selected in this way in order to realize one semantic choice.

Where there are alternatives, such that a given semantic option is realized EITHER by this OR by that set of features in the grammar, these are often determined by the environment. For instance, the grammar of personal medicine—the language used to describe one's ailments—is not the same in the doctor's consulting room as it is in a family or neighbourhood context: compare *I've got the most terrible tummy ache* with *my digestion's troubling me* as realizations of some meaning such as 'intensity and location of pain'. The environment is generally the higher-level environment, either the immediate paradigmatic environment—that is, the other options that are being selected at the same time—or the social context as a whole.

Sometimes, however, the alternatives are not environmentally conditioned but appear initially as free variants, as simply alternative grammatical realizations of one and the same semantic choice. It may be that they are; it would be rash to pretend that there is no free variation in language. But in the grammatical realization of semantic options the alternatives usually turn out to represent more delicate semantic choices. In other words, there *is* a difference in meaning, although it is not so fundamental as the grammatical distinction would suggest (and therefore one begins by putting the two grammatical forms together as 'having the same meaning'). This is a very general and important phenomenon and we have already seen it illustrated more than once. For instance, three forms of conditional threat:

> if you do that again I'll smack you
> do that again and I'll smack you
> don't do that again or I'll smack you

When one has made the point that all these are possible realizations of the semantic option of 'threat', one tends to be satisfied and to stop there, saying merely 'these all have the same meaning'. But they have not the same meaning. They are all threats, and they represent the same semantic options *up to a point*—which means, here, up to a particular point in delicacy. But they are not free variants. There is a more subtle distinction between them, and this is shown by the fact that they realize more delicate sub-options in the semantic network.

One question that has been left out of consideration here, is this. It is necessary to recognize 'semantic structures'? In explaining grammar, and in moving from grammar to phonology, we cannot account for everything simply by letting the grammatical networks wire into (pre-select in) the phonological ones and delaying the formation of structures until the phonological stratum. We have to set up structures at the grammatical level. This is simply because, for most of the options in the grammar, it is not possible to specify their 'output' directly in terms of phonological options. We can do this in the case of those realized by tone, cited above; these are realized directly by choices in the phonology. But we could not handle, for example, the grammatical system of mood in this way. For this, as for the majority of grammatical systems, we have to state the realization first in terms of configurations of functions—that is, of grammatical structures.

Similarly, in going from phonology to phonetics we set up

phonological structures, such as syllable and foot, which are likewise configurations of functions.

By analogy, therefore, the question arises whether we need semantic structures as well (cf. Lamb, 1970).

It is important to emphasize here that structure is defined as the 'configuration of functions', since this is abstract enough to cover semantic structure if such a thing is to be formulated. The shape of a structure may vary; we may express it lineally or hierarchically or simultaneously. But all such shapes have in common the property of being configurations of functions.

The same would apply to semantic structures. Lamb suggested at one time (cf. Fleming, 1969) that semantic structures were networks, grammatical (syntactic) structures were trees (hierarchical), morphological structures strings (linear) and phonological structures bundles (simultaneous). In the present account, grammatical and phonological structures are both trees composed of hierarchies of strings; but it remains the case that semantic structures need by no means have the same shape as structures at any other level. All that the term 'structure' implies is that there will be some configurations of functions at that stratum, and that these will realize the meaning selections, the combinations of options in the meaning potential.

The combination of system and structure with rank leads to a fairly abstract grammar (fairly 'deep', in the Chomskyan sense) and enables us to specify fairly accurately in theoretical terms— though not of course in rule-of-thumb terms—just how abstract it is. In principle, a grammatical system is as abstract (is as 'semantic') as possible given only that it can generate integrated structures; that is, that its output can be expressed in terms of functions which can be mapped directly on to other functions, the result being a single structural 'shape' (though one which is of course multiply labelled). This is already fairly abstract, and it may be unnecessary therefore to interpose another layer of structure between the semantic systems and the grammatical systems—given the limited purpose of the semantic systems, which is to account for the meaning potential associated with defined social contexts and settings.

On the other hand it is possible that one might be able to handle more complex areas of behaviour by means of a concept of semantic structure. It may be, for instance, that the study of institutional communication networks, such as the chain of command or the patterns of consultation and negotiation in an industrial concern, might be extended to a linguistic analysis if the semantic options were first represented in semantic structures —since the options themselves could then be made more abstract. Various complex decision-making strategies in groups of different sizes might become accessible to linguistic observation in the same way. But for the moment this remains a matter of speculation. Sociological semantics is still at a rather elementary stage, and the contexts that have been investigated, which are some of those most likely to be significant in relation to socialization and social learning, are fairly closely circumscribed and seem to be describable by direct pre-selection between semantic and grammatical systems.

7. Uses of language, and 'macro-functions'

These networks are what we understand by 'semantics'. They constitute a stratum that is intermediate between the social system and the grammatical system. The former is wholly outside language, the latter is wholly within language; the semantic networks, which describe the range of alternative meanings available to the speaker in given social contexts and settings, form a bridge between the two.

Like any other level of representation in a stratal pattern, they face both ways. Here, the downward relation is with the grammar; but the upward relation is with the extra-linguistic context.

If we have tended to stress the instrumentality of linguistics, rather than its autonomy, this reflects our concern with language as meaning potential in behavioural settings. In investigating grammar and phonology, linguists have tended to insist on the autonomy of their subject; this is natural and useful, since these are the 'inner' strata of the linguistic system, the core of language so to speak, and in their immediate context they are 'autonomous' —they do not relate directly outside language. But they are in turn contingent on other systems which do relate outside language. Moreover we take the view that we can understand the nature of the inner stratal systems of language only if we do attempt to relate language to extra-linguistic phenomena.

Let us turn for a moment to the language of the very young child. At an early stage, it is possible to postulate very small proto-linguistic systems in which the 'grammar' relates directly to the function for which language is being used. For example, in an item such as *byebye mummy* the structure is a direct reflection of the meaning of the utterance: the structure is a configuration of Valediction and Person, and it represents just such options in the child's potential for verbal interaction with his parents. Here grammar and semantics are one.

At this stage the child has acquired a small set of functions or uses of language within each of which he has certain options, a range of meanings open to him. These meanings are expressed through rather simple structures whose elements derive directly from the functions themselves:

	functions	options			structures		items
form of representation		$a\!\!-\!\!\begin{array}{l}b\\c\end{array}$ ('if a, then either b or c')		$\begin{array}{c}n\\ \underline{\quad\quad}\\ p\quad\quad q\end{array}$	('n consists of p followed by q')		(text)
example	i n t e r a c t i o n a l	valedic-tion V	general (1) V:byebye / bedtime (2) V:nightnight	(i) | Valediction			byebye (1, 3) nightnight (2, 3)
		destina-tion	non-person-alized (3) / person-alized (4) + P:mummy	(ii) Valediction + Person			byebye mummy (1, 4) nightnight mummy (2, 4)

Note: This example is invented. For examples drawn from an actual description of a child's linguistic system, see Figures 1–3 in Paper 2.

Here there is no need to distinguish between functions and uses of language, or between grammar and semantics.

This situation might represent an early stage in the evolution of human language; we do not know.

In the individual, as time goes on, the situations and settings in which language is used become more varied and complex, and the meaning potential associated with them becomes richer. We can no longer write a simple description in which the structure relates directly to the function and 'function' equals 'use'.

Instead, the picture is something like this. We could list indefinitely many 'uses of language'. There are innumerable types of situation in which language plays a part, and innumerable purposes which the speaker makes language serve. It is a useful exercise just to think about these and attempt to categorize them from one's own experience; but this will not by itself provide a systematic basis for understanding grammar.

89

Some of these uses can be systematized into social contexts and settings with at least partially specifiable behaviour potential associated with them. There are uses of language, such as those we have been exemplifying, in which some definable range of alternatives is open to the speaker and these are realized through language. Here we can specify, up to a point, the set of possible meanings that can be expressed.

In a few instances these are like the meanings of the child's proto-language, in that they can be related directly to grammatical structures, as is often the case in the language used in games. Sometimes we would not even need to postulate a structure—we could go straight to the actual words and phrases used. Normally, however, we have to relate the meanings first to systematic selections within the grammar, from which the grammatical structures are then in turn derived.

That is to say, we relate the semantic systems to grammatical systems, regarding them as a form of 'pre-selection', as illustrated in the last section. A choice in the semantics 'pre-selects' an option in the grammar, or a set of such options.

But what is the nature and origin of the grammatical system? Grammar is the level of formal organization in language; it is a purely internal level of organization, and is in fact the main defining characteristic of language. But it is not arbitrary. Grammar evolved as 'content form': as a representation of the meaning potential through which language serves its various social functions. The grammar itself has a functional basis.

What has happened in the course of the evolution of language—and this is no more than a reasonable assumption, corresponding to what happens in the development of language in the individual—is that the demands made on language have constantly expanded, and the language system has been shaped accordingly. There has been an increase in the complexity of linguistic function, and the complexity of language has increased with it. Most significantly, this has meant the emergence of the stratal form of organization, with a purely formal level of coding at its core. This performs the function of integrating the very complex meaning selections into single integrated structures. The way it does this is by sorting out the many very specific uses of language into a small number of highly general functions which underlie them all (cf. Halliday, in press).

We thus need to make a distinction, in the adult language system, between 'function' and 'use', a distinction which was

90

unnecessary in the case of the child's proto-language. With the child, each use of language has its own grammar from which we can (in the idealized original state of the system) fully derive the structures and items employed in that use. Our example *byebye mummy!* could be described entirely in terms of the grammar of the 'interactional' use of language.

With the adult this is not so. He may use language in a vast number of different ways, in different types of situation and for different purposes; but we cannot identify a finite set of uses and write a grammar for each of them. What we can identify, however, is a finite set of functions—let us call them 'macro-functions' to make the distinction clearer—which are general to all these uses and through which the meaning potential associated with them is encoded into grammatical structures.

These 'macro-functions' have been recognized for a long time in 'functional' theories of language (for this reason we retain the name 'function' for them). By using the notion of a grammatical system, we can show more clearly how they are embodied in the grammar, where they appear as relatively discrete areas of formalized meaning potential, or in other words relatively independent sets of options. We referred to these as 'functional components' of the grammar.

Three principal components can be recognized, under the headings 'ideational', 'interpersonal' and 'textual'. The ideational component is that part of the grammar concerned with the expression of experience, including both the processes within and beyond the self—the phenomena of the external world and those of consciousness—and the logical relations deducible from them. The ideational component thus has two sub-components, the experiential and the logical. The interpersonal component is the grammar of personal participation; it expresses the speaker's role in the speech situation, his personal commitment and his interaction with others. The textual component is concerned with the creation of text; it expresses the structure of information, and the relation of each part of the discourse to the whole and to the setting.

We now need to relate these 'macro-functions' to what the adult does with language. (By 'adult' we mean someone who has developed the mature language system, as distinct from the child's proto-language referred to earlier.) The adult engages in a great variety of uses of language, which in themselves are unsystematized and vague. We attempt to impose some order on them, by

91

identifying social contexts and settings for which we can state the meaning potential in a systematic way. But he does not have a different grammar for each of them. He has just one and the same grammar, which is called on in different ways and of which now one part is emphasized and now another.

The macro-functions are the most general categories of meaning potential, common to all uses of language. With only minor exceptions, whatever the speaker is doing with language he will draw on all these components of the grammar. He will need to make some reference to the categories of his own experience—in other words, the language will be *about* something. He will need to take up some position in the speech situation; at the very least he will specify his own communication role and set up expectations for that of the hearer—in terms of statement, question, response and the like. And what he says will be structured as 'text'—that is to say, it will be operational in the given context. These are properties of nearly all acts of communication; by and large, every text unit is the product of options of these three kinds. It is not surprising therefore that these form the fundamental components of the grammar, since it is grammar that turns meanings into text.

This is just another way of saying that it is through its organization into functional components that the formal system of languages is linked to language use. When we say that the realization of meaning potential—of options in semantics—is through the pre-selection of options in the grammar, this means in fact pre-selection within these functional components. The options in semantics depend on social context and setting, which are extra-linguistic factors. The options in the grammar are organized into general components which are internal to language. But these components are based on 'macro-functions' that are extra-linguistic in origin and orientation. In the evolution of language as a whole, the form of language has been determined by the functions it has to serve.

We said earlier that the input to the semantics was social and specific, whereas its output was linguistic and general. We can now try and clarify this a little. It was not meant to imply that the social contexts and settings themselves are highly specific categories; in fact they are very general. But the range of alternatives which each one offers, the meaning potential available to the speaker in a given situation type, tends to be specific to the situation type in question; whereas the grammatical options through which the meaning selections are realized are general to the language as a whole. In other words, the move from GENERAL social categories to GENERAL linguistic categories involves an intermediate level of SPECIFIC categorization where the one is related to the other. An 'interface' of more specific features is needed to bridge the gap from the generalizations of sociology to those of linguistics.

Let us attempt a pictorial representation of what we have been saying.

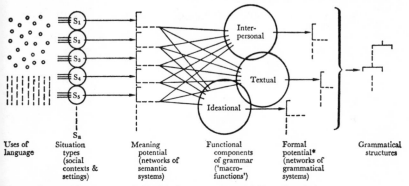

| Uses of language | Situation types (social contexts & settings) | Meaning potential (networks of semantic systems) | Functional components of grammar ('macro-functions') | Formal potential* (networks of grammatical systems) | Grammatical structures |

* i.e. meaning potential at the grammatical level, in the system-structure definition of 'meaning'.

An amorphous and indeterminate set of 'uses of language' is partly reducible to generalized situation types, the social contexts and behavioural settings in which language functions. For any one of these situation types, we seek to identify a meaning potential, the range of alternatives open to the speaker in the context of that situation type; these are expressed as semantic networks within which meaning selections are made. The options in the semantic network determine the choice of linguistic forms by 'pre-selection' of particular options within the functional components of the grammar. These grammatical options are realized in integrated structures formed by the mapping on to one another of configurations of elements derived from each of the 'macro-functions'.

This paper was first published in *Working Papers and Prepublications* (series C, no. 14), Centro Internazionale di Semiotica e di Linguistica, Università di Urbino, 1972.

REFERENCES

Fleming, Ilah (1969). 'Stratificational theory: an annotated bibliography', *Journal of English Linguistics*, **3.**

Halliday, Michael A. K. 'Learning how to mean', in Eric and Elizabeth Lenneberg (eds.), *Foundations of language development: a multidisciplinary approach*, UNESCO & International Brain Research Organization. In press.

Lamb, Sydney M. (1970). 'Linguistic and cognitive networks', in Paul Garvin (ed.), *Cognition: a multiple view*, New York, Spartan Books.

Mitchell, T. F. (1951). 'The language of buying and selling in Cyrenaica', *Hesperis*.

5 Linguistic function and literary style:

an inquiry into the language of William Golding's *The Inheritors*

My main concern, in this paper, is with criteria of relevance. This, it seems to me, is one of the central problems in the study of 'style in language': I mean the problem of distinguishing between mere linguistic regularity, which in itself is of no interest to literary studies, and regularity which is significant for the poem or prose work in which we find it. I remember an entertaining paper read to the Philological Society in Cambridge some years ago, by Professor John Sinclair, in which he drew our attention to some very striking linguistic patterns displayed in the poetry of William McGonagall, and invited us to say why, if this highly structured language was found in what we all agreed was such very trivial poetry, we should be interested in linguistic regularities at all. It is no new discovery to say that pattern in language does not by itself make literature, still less 'good literature': nothing is more regular than the rhythm of *Three Blind Mice*, and if this is true of phonological regularities it is likely to be true also of syntactic ones. But we lack general criteria for determining whether any particular instance of linguistic prominence is likely to be stylistically relevant or not.

This is not a simple matter, and any discussion of it is bound to touch on more than one topic, or at the least to adopt more than one angle of vision. Moreover the line of approach will often, inevitably, be indirect, and the central concern may at times be lost sight of round some of the corners. It seems to me necessary, first of all, to discuss and to emphasize the place of semantics in the study of style; and this in turn will lead to a consideration of 'functional' theories of language and their relevance for the student of literature. At the same time these general points need to be exemplified; and here I have allowed the illustration to take over the stage: when I re-examined for this purpose a novel I had first studied some four years ago, *The Inheritors* by William Golding, there seemed to be so much that was of interest in its own right. I do not think there is any antithesis between the 'textual' and the 'theoretical' in the study of language, so I hope the effect of this may be to strengthen rather than to weaken the general argument. The discussion of *The Inheritors*, which takes up much of the paper, may be seen either in relation to just that one work or in relation to a general theory; I am not sure that it is possible to separate these two perspectives, either from each other or from various intermediate fields of attention such as an author, a genre or a literary tradition.

The paper will fall into four parts: first, a discussion of a 'functional theory of language'; second, a reference to various questions raised at the first 'Style in Language' conference and in other current writings; third, an examination of certain features of the language of *The Inheritors;* and fourth, a brief résumé on the question of stylistic relevance.

*   *   *

The term *function* is used, in two distinct though related senses, at two very different points in the description of language. First, it is used in the sense of 'grammatical (or 'syntactic') function', to refer to elements of linguistic structures such as actor and goal or subject and object or theme and rheme. These 'functions' are the roles occupied by classes of words, phrases and the like in the structure of higher units. Secondly, it is used to refer to the 'functions' of language as a whole: for example in the well-known work of Karl Bühler in which he proposed a three-way division of language function into the representational, the conative and the expressive.

Here I am using 'function' in the second sense; referring, however, not specifically to Bühler's theory, but to the generalized notion of 'functions of language'. By a functional theory of language I mean one which attempts to explain linguistic structure, and linguistic phenomena, by reference to the notion that language plays a certain part in our lives; that it is required to serve certain universal types of demand. I find this approach valuable in general for the insight it gives into the nature and use of language, but particularly so in the context of stylistic studies.

The demands that we make on language, as speakers and writers, listeners and readers, are indefinitely many and varied. They can be derived, ultimately, from a small number of very general headings; but what these headings are will depend on what questions we are asking. For example, if we were to take a broadly psychological viewpoint, and consider the functions that language serves in the life of the individual, we might arrive at some such scheme as Bühler's, referred to above. If on the other hand we asked a more sociological type of question, concerning the functions that language serves in the life of the community, we should probably elaborate some framework such as Malinowski's distinction into a pragmatic and a magical function.[1] Many others could be suggested besides.

These questions are extrinsic to language; and the categorizations of language function that depend on them are of interest because and to the extent that the questions themselves are of interest. Such categorizations therefore imply a strictly instrumental view of linguistic theory. Some would perhaps reject this on the grounds that it does not admit the autonomy of linguistics and linguistic investigations. I am not myself impressed by that argument, although I would stress that any one particular instrumental view is by itself inadequate as a general characteristic of language. But a purely extrinsic theory of language functions does fail to take into account one thing, namely the fact that the multiplicity of function, if the idea is valid at all, is likely to be reflected somewhere in the internal organization of language itself. If language is, as it were, programmed to serve a variety of needs, then this should show up in some way in an investigation of linguistic structure.

In fact this functional plurality is very clearly built in to the structure of language, and forms the basis of its semantic and 'syntactic' (i.e. grammatical and lexical) organization. If we set up a functional framework that is neutral as to external emphasis, but designed to take into account the nature of the internal, semantic and syntactic patterns of language, we arrive at something that is very suggestive for literary studies, because it represents a general characterization of semantic functions—of the meaning potential of the language system. Let me suggest here the framework that seems to me most helpful. It is a rather simple catalogue of three basic functions, one of which has two subheadings.

In the first place language serves for the expression of content: it has a representational, or, as I would prefer to call it, an *ideational* function. (This is sometimes referred to as the expression of 'cognitive meaning', though I find the term *cognitive* misleading;

97

there is after all a cognitive element in all linguistic functions.) Two points need to be emphasized concerning this ideational function of language. The first is that it is through this function that the speaker or writer embodies in language his experience of the phenomena of the real world; and this includes his experience of the internal world of his own consciousness: his reactions, cognitions and perceptions, and also his linguistic acts of speaking and understanding. We shall in no sense be adopting an extreme pseudo-Whorfian position (I say 'pseudo-'Whorfian because Whorf himself never was extreme) if we add that, in serving this function, language lends structure to his experience and helps to determine his way of looking at things. The speaker can see through and around the settings of his semantic system; but he is aware that, in doing so, he is seeing reality in a new light, like Alice in Looking-glass House. There is, however, and this is the second point, one component of ideational meaning which, while not unrelatable to experience, is nevertheless organized in language in a way which marks it off as distinct: this is the expression of certain fundamental logical relations such as are encoded in language in the form of co-ordination, apposition, modification and the like. The notion of co-ordination, for example, as in *sun, moon and stars*, can be derived from an aspect of the speaker's experience; but this and other such relations are realized through the medium of a particular type of structural mechanism (that of linear recursion) which takes them, linguistically, out of the domain of experience to form a functionally neutral, 'logical' component in the total spectrum of meanings. Within the ideational function of language, therefore, we can recognize two sub-functions, the *experiential* and the *logical;* and the distinction is a significant one for our present purpose.

In the second place, language serves what we may call an *interpersonal* function. This is quite different from the expression of content. Here, the speaker is using language as the means of his own intrusion into the speech event: the expression of his comments, his attitudes and evaluations, and also of the relationship that he sets up between himself and the listener—in particular, the communication role that he adopts, of informing, questioning, greeting, persuading and the like. The interpersonal function thus subsumes both the expressive and the conative, which are not in fact distinct in the linguistic system: to give one example, the meanings 'I do not know' (expressive) and 'you tell me' (conative) are combined in a single semantic feature, that of question,

98

typically expressed in the grammar by an interrogative; the interrogative is both expressive and conative at the same time. The set of communication roles is unique among social relations in that it is brought into being and maintained solely through language. But the interpersonal element in language extends beyond what we might think of as its rhetorical functions. In the wider context, language is required to serve in the establishment and maintenance of all human relationships; it is the means whereby social groups are integrated and the individual is identified and reinforced. It is I think significant for certain forms of literature that, since personality is dependent on interaction which is in turn mediated through language, the 'interpersonal' function in language is both interactional and personal: there is, in other words, a component in language which serves at one and the same time to express both the inner and the outer surfaces of the individual, as a single undifferentiated area of meaning potential that is personal in the broadest sense.

These two functions, the ideational and the interpersonal, may seem sufficiently all-embracing; and in the context of an instrumental approach to language they are. But there is a third function which is in turn instrumental to these two, whereby language is as it were enabled to meet the demands that are made on it; I shall call this the *textual* function, since it is concerned with the creation of text. It is a function internal to language, and for this reason is not usually taken into account where the objects of investigation are extrinsic; but it came to be specifically associated with the term 'functional' in the work of the Prague scholars who developed Bühler's ideas within the framework of a linguistic theory (cf. their terms 'functional syntax', 'functional sentence perspective'). It is through this function that language makes links with itself and with the situation; and discourse becomes possible, because the speaker or writer can produce a text and the listener or reader can recognize one. A *text* is an operational unit of language, as a sentence is a syntactic unit; it may be spoken or written, long or short; and it includes as a special instance a literary text, whether haiku or Homeric epic. It is the text and not some super-sentence that is the relevant unit for stylistic studies; this is a functional-semantic concept and is not definable by size. And therefore the 'textual' function is not limited to the establishment of relations between sentences; it is concerned just as much with the internal organization of the sentence, with its meaning as a message both in itself and in relation to the context.

A tentative categorization of the principal elements of English syntax in terms of the above functions is given in Table 1 (p. 141). This table is intended to serve a twofold purpose. In the first place, it will help to make more concrete the present concept of a functional theory, by showing how the various functions are realized through the grammatical systems of the language, all of which are accounted for in this way. Not all the labels may be self-explanatory, nor is the framework so compartmental as in this bare outline it is made to seem: there is a high degree of indeterminacy in the fuller picture, representing the indeterminacy that is present throughout language, in its categories and its relations, its types and its tokens. Secondly, it will bring out the fact that the syntax of a language is organized in such a way that it expresses as a whole the range of linguistic functions, but that the symptoms of functional diversity are not to be sought in single sentences or sentence types. In general, that is to say, we shall not find whole sentences or even smaller structures having just one function. Typically each sentence embodies all functions, though one or another may be more prominent; and most constituents of sentences also embody more than one function, through their ability to combine two or more syntactic roles.

Let us introduce an example at this point. Here is a well-known passage from *Through the Looking-glass, and what Alice found there*:

'I don't understand you,' said Alice. 'It's dreadfully confusing!'
'That's the effect of living backwards,' the Queen said kindly: 'it always makes one a little giddy at first—'
'Living backwards!' Alice repeated in great astonishment. 'I never heard of such a thing!'
'—but there's one great advantage in it, that one's memory works both ways.'
'I'm sure *mine* only works one way,' Alice remarked. 'I can't remember things before they happen.'
'It's a poor sort of memory that only works backwards,' the Queen remarked.
'What sort of things do *you* remember best?' Alice ventured to ask.
'Oh, things that happened the week after next,' the Queen replied in a careless tone.

To illustrate the last point first, namely that most constituents of sentences embody more than one function, by combining different syntactic roles: the constituent *what sort of things* occupies simultaneously the syntactic roles of 'theme', of 'phenomenon' (that is, object of cognition, perception etc.) and of 'interrogation point'. The theme represents a particular status in the message, and is thus an expression of 'textual' function: it is the speaker's point of departure. If the speaker is asking a question he usually, in English, takes the request for information as his theme, expressing this by putting the question phrase first; here therefore the same element is both theme and interrogation point—the latter being an expression of 'interpersonal' function since it defines the specific communication roles the speaker has chosen for himself and for the listener: the speaker is behaving as questioner. Thirdly, *what sort of thing* is the phenomenon dependent on the mental process *remember;* and this concept of a mental phenomenon, as something that can be talked about, is an expression of the 'ideational' function of language—of language as content, relatable to the speaker's and the listener's experience. It should be emphasized that it is not, in fact, the syntactic role in isolation, but the structure of which it forms a part, that is semantically significant: it is not the theme, for example, but the total theme-rheme structure which contributes to the texture of the discourse.

Thus the constituents themselves tend to be multivalent; which is another way of saying that the very notion of a constituent is itself rather too concrete to be of much help in a functional context. A constituent is a particular word or phrase in a particular place; but functionally the choice of an item may have one meaning, its repetition another and its location in structure yet another—or many others, as we have seen. So, in the Queen's remark, *it's a poor sort of memory that only works backwards*, the word *poor* is a 'modifier', and thus expresses a sub-class of its head word *memory* (ideational); while at the same time it is an 'epithet' expressing the Queen's attitude (interpersonal), and the choice of this word in this environment (as opposed to, say, *useful*) indicates more specifically that the attitude is one of disapproval. The words *it's . . . that* have here no reference at all outside the sentence, but they structure the message in a particular way (textual) which represents the Queen's opinion as if it was an 'attribute' (ideational); and defines one class of *memory* as exclusively possessing this undesirable quality (ideational). The lexical repetition in *memory that only works backwards* relates the Queen's remark (textual) to *mine only works one way*, in which *mine* refers anaphorically, by ellipsis, to *memory* in the preceding sentence (textual) and also to *I* in Alice's expression of her own judgment *I'm sure* (interpersonal). Thus ideational content and personal

101

interaction are woven together with and by means of the textual structure to form a coherent whole.

Taking a somewhat broader perspective, we again find the same interplay of functions. The ideational meaning of the passage is enshrined in the phrase *living backwards*; we have a general characterization of the nature of experience, in which *things that happened the week after next* turns out to be an acceptable sentence. (I am not suggesting it is serious, or offering a deep literary interpretation; I am merely using it to illustrate the nature of language.) On the interpersonal level the language expresses, through a pattern of question (or exclamation) and response, a basic relationship of seeker and guide, in interplay with various other paired functions such as yours and mine, for and against, child and adult, wonderment and judgment. The texture is that of dialogue in narrative, within which the Queen's complex thematic structures (e.g. *there's one great advantage to it, that . . .*) contrast with the much simpler (i.e. linguistically unmarked) message patterns used by Alice.

A functional theory of language is a theory about meanings, not about words or constructions; we shall not attempt to assign a word or a construction directly to one function or another. Where then do we find the functions differentiated in language? They are differentiated semantically, as different areas of what I called the 'meaning potential'. Language is itself a potential: it is the totality of what the speaker can do. (By 'speaker' I mean always the language user, whether as speaker, listener, writer or reader: *homo grammaticus*, in fact.) We are considering, as it were, the dynamics of the semantic strategies that are available to him. If we represent the language system in this way, as networks of interrelated options which define, as a whole, the resources for what the speaker wants to say, we find empirically that these options fall into a small number of fairly distinct sets. In the last resort, every option in language is related to every other; there are no completely independent choices. But the total network of meaning potential is actually composed of a number of smaller networks, each one highly complex in itself but related to the others in a way that is relatively simple: rather like an elaborate piece of circuitry made up of two or three complex blocks of wiring with fairly simple interconnections. Each of these blocks corresponds to one of the functions of language.

In Table 1, where the columns represent our linguistic functions, each column is one 'block' of options. These blocks are to be

102

thought of as wired 'in parallel'. That is to say, the speaker does not first think of the content of what he wants to say and then go on to decide what kind of a message it is and where he himself comes into it—whether it will be statement or question, what modalities are involved and the like.[2] All these functions, the ideational, the interpersonal and the textual, are simultaneously embodied in his planning procedures. (If we pursue the metaphor, it is the rows of the table that are wired 'in series': they represent the hierarchy of constituents in the grammar, where the different functions come together. Each row is one constituent type, and is a point of intersection of options from the different columns.)

The linguistic differentiation among the ideational, interpersonal and textual functions is thus to be found in the way in which choices in meaning are interrelated to one another. Each function defines a set of options that is relatively—though only relatively—independent of the other sets. Dependence here refers to the degree of mutual determination: one part of the content of what one says tends to exert a considerable effect on other parts of the content, whereas one's attitudes and speech roles are relatively undetermined by it: the speaker is, by and large, free to associate any interpersonal meanings with any content. What I wish to stress here is that all types of option, from whatever function they are derived, are meaningful. At every point the speaker is selecting among a range of possibilities that differ in meaning; and if we attempt to separate meaning from choice we are turning a valuable distinction (between linguistic functions) into an arbitrary dichotomy (between 'meaningful' and 'meaningless' choices). All options are embedded in the language system: the system is a network of options, deriving from all the various functions of language. If we take the useful functional distinction of 'ideational' and 'interpersonal' and rewrite it, under the labels 'cognitive' and 'expressive', in such a way as sharply to separate the two, equating cognitive with meaning and expressive with style, we not only fail to recognize the experiential basis of many of our own intuitions about works of literature and their impact —style as the expression of what the thing is about, at some level; my own illustration in this paper is one example of this—but we also attach the contrasting status of 'non-cognitive' (whatever this may mean) to precisely those options that seem best to embody our conception of a work of literature, those whereby the writer gives form to the discourse and expresses his own individuality. Even if we are on our guard against the implication

103

that the regions of language in which style resides are the ones which are linguistically non-significant, we are still drawing the wrong line. There are no regions of language in which style does not reside.

We should not in fact be drawing lines at all; the boundaries on our map consist only in shading and overlapping. Nevertheless they are there; and provided we are not forced into seeking an unreal distinction between the 'what' and the 'how', we can show, by reference to the generalized notion of linguistic functions, how such real contrasts as that of denotation and connotation relate to the functional map of language as a whole, and thus how they may be incorporated into the linguistic study of style. It is through this chain of reasoning that we may hope to establish criteria of relevance, and to demonstrate the connection between the syntactic observations which we make about a text and the nature of the impact which that text has upon us. If we can relate the linguistic patterns (grammatical, lexical and even phonological) to the underlying functions of language, we have a criterion for eliminating what is trivial and for distinguishing true foregrounding from mere prominence of a statistical or an absolute kind.

Foregrounding, as I understand it, is prominence that is motivated. It is not difficult to find patterns of prominence in a poem or prose text, regularities in the sounds or words or structures that stand out in some way, or may be brought out by careful reading; and one may often be led in this way towards a new insight, through finding that such prominence contributes to the writer's total meaning. But unless it does, it will seem to lack motivation; a feature that is brought into prominence will be 'foregrounded' only if it relates to the meaning of the text as a whole. This relationship is a functional one: if a particular feature of the language contributes, by its prominence, to the total meaning of the work it does so by virtue of and through the medium of its own value in the language—through the linguistic function from which its meaning is derived. Where that function is relevant to our interpretation of the work, the prominence will appear as motivated. I shall try to illustrate this by reference to *The Inheritors*. First, however, a few remarks, about some points raised at the earlier conference and in subsequent discussions, which I hope will make slightly more explicit the context within which Golding's work is being examined.

*　　　*　　　*

There are three questions I should like to touch on: Is prominence to be regarded as a departure from or as the attainment of a norm? To what extent is prominence a quantitative effect, to be uncovered or at least stated by means of statistics? How real is the distinction between prominence that is due to subject matter and prominence that is due to something else? All three questions are very familiar, and my justification for bringing them up once more is not that what I have to say about them is new but rather that some partial answers are needed if we are attempting an integrated approach to language and style, and that these answers will be pertinent to a consideration of our main question, which is that of criteria of relevance.

I have used the term *prominence* as a general name for the phenomenon of linguistic highlighting, whereby some feature of the language of a text stands out in some way. In choosing this term I hoped to avoid the assumption that a linguistic feature which is brought under attention will always be seen as a departure. It is quite natural to characterize such prominence as departure from a norm, since this explains why it is remarkable, especially if one is stressing the subjective nature of the highlighting effect; thus Leech, discussing what he refers to as 'schemes' that is, 'foregrounded patterns . . . in grammar or phonology', writes 'It is ultimately a matter of subjective judgment whether . . . the regularity seems remarkable enough to constitute a definite departure from the normal functions of language'.[3] But at the same time it is often objected, not unreasonably, that the 'departure' view puts too high a value on oddness, and suggests that normal forms are of no interest in the study of style. Thus Wellek: 'The danger of linguistic stylistics is its focus on deviations from, and distortions of, the linguistic norm. We get a kind of counter-grammar, a science of discards. Normal stylistics is abandoned to the grammarian, and deviational stylistics is reserved for the student of literature. But often the most commonplace, the most normal, linguistic elements are the constituents of literary structure.'[4]

Two kinds of answer have been given to this objection. One is that there are two types of prominence, only one of which is negative, a departure from a norm; the other is positive, and is the attainment or the establishment of a norm. The second is that departure may in any case be merely statistical: we are concerned not only with deviations, ungrammatical forms, but also with what we may call 'deflections', departures from some expected pattern of frequency.

The distinction between negative and positive prominence, or departures and regularities, is drawn by Leech, who contrasts foregrounding in the form of 'motivated deviation from linguistic, or other socially accepted norms' with foregrounding applied to 'the opposite circumstance, in which a writer temporarily renounces his permitted freedom of choice, introducing uniformity where there would normally be diversity'. Strictly speaking this is not an 'opposite circumstance', since if diversity is normal then uniformity is a deviation. But where there is uniformity there is regularity; and this can be treated as a positive feature, as the establishment of a norm. Thus, to quote Hymes, '. . . in some "sources", especially poets, style may not be deviation from but achievement of a norm'.[5]

However, this is not a distinction between two types of prominence; it is a distinction between two ways of looking at prominence, depending on the standpoint of the observer. There is no single universally relevant norm, no one set of expectancies to which all instances may be referred. On the one hand, there are differences of perspective. The text may be seen as 'part' of a larger 'whole', such as the author's complete works, or the tradition to which it belongs, so that what is globally a departure may be locally a norm. The expectancies may lie in 'the language as a whole', in a diatypic variety or register[6] characteristic of some situation type (Osgood's 'situational norms'),[7] in a genre or literary form, or in some special institution such as the Queen's Christmas message; we always have the choice of saying either 'this departs from a pattern' or 'this forms a pattern'. On the other hand, there are differences of attention. The text may be seen as 'this' in contrast with 'that', with another poem or another novel; stylistic studies are essentially comparative in nature, and either may be taken as the point of departure. As Hymes says, there are egalitarian universes, comprising sets of norms, and 'it would be arbitrary to choose one norm as a standard from which the others depart'. It may be more helpful to look at any given instance of prominence in one way rather than in the other, sometimes as departure from a norm and sometimes as the attainment of a norm; but there is only one type of phenomenon here, not two.

There is perhaps a limiting case, the presence of one ungrammatical sentence in an entire poem or novel; presumably this could be viewed only as a departure. But in itself it would be unlikely to be of any interest. Deviation, the use of ungrammatical forms, has received a great deal of attention, and seems to be regarded, at times, as prominence *par excellence*. This is probably because it is a deterministic concept. Deviant forms are actually prohibited by the rules of whatever is taken to be the norm; or, to express it positively, the norm that is established by a set of deviant forms excludes all texts but the one in which they occur. But for this very reason deviation is of very limited interest in stylistics. It is rarely found; and when it is found, it is often not relevant. On the contrary; if we follow McIntosh (who finds it 'a chastening thought'), '. . . quite often where the impact of an entire work may be enormous, yet word by word, phrase by phrase, clause by clause, sentence by sentence, there may seem to be nothing very unusual or arresting, in grammar or in vocabulary . . .'.[8]

Hence the very reasonable supposition that prominence may be of a probabilistic kind, defined by Bloch as 'frequency distributions and transitional probabilities [which] differ from those . . . in the language as a whole'.[9] This is what we have referred to above as 'deflection'. It too may be viewed either as departure from a norm or as its attainment. If, for example, we meet seven occurrences of a rather specific grammatical pattern, such as that cited by Leech '*my* + noun + *you* + verb', a norm has been set up and there is, or may be, a strong local expectancy that an eighth will follow; the probability of finding this pattern repeated in eight successive clauses is infinitesimally small, so that the same phenomenon constitutes a departure. It is fairly easy to see that the one always implies the other; the contravention of one expectation is at the same time the fulfilment of a different one. Either way, whether the prominence is said to consist in law-breaking or in law-making, we are dealing with a type of phenomenon that is expressible in quantitative terms, to which statistical concepts may be applied.

In the context of stylistic investigations, the term 'statistical' may refer to anything from a highly detailed measurement of the reactions of subjects to sets of linguistic variables, to the parenthetical insertion of figures of occurrences designed to explain why a particular feature is being singled out for discussion. What is common to all these is the assumption that numerical data on language may be stylistically significant; whatever subsequent operations are performed, there has nearly always been some counting of linguistic elements in the text, whether of phonological units or words or grammatical patterns, and the figures obtained are potentially an indication of prominence. The notion that prominence may be defined statistically is still not always accepted; there seem to be two main counter-arguments, but whatever substance these may have as stated they are not, I think, valid objections to the point at issue. The first is essentially that, since style is a manifestation of the individual, it cannot be reduced to counting. This is true, but, as has often been said before, it misses the point. If there is such a thing as a recognizable style, whether of a work, an author, or an entire period or literary tradition, its distinctive quality can in the last analysis be stated in terms of relative frequencies, although the linguistic features that show significant variation may be simple and obvious or extremely subtle and complex. An example of how period styles may be revealed in this way will be found in Josephine Miles' 'Eras in English poetry', in which she shows that different periods are characterized by a distinction in the dominant type of sentence structure, that between 'the sort which emphasizes substantival elements—the phrasal and co-ordinative modifications of subject and object—and the sort which emphasizes clausal co-ordination and complication of the predicate'.[10]

The second objection is that numbers of occurrences must be irrelevant to style because we are not aware of frequency in language and therefore cannot respond to it. This is almost certainly not true. We are probably rather sensitive to the relative frequency of different grammatical and lexical patterns, which is an aspect of 'meaning potential'; and our expectancies, as readers, are in part based on our awareness of the probabilities inherent in the language. This is what enables us to grasp the new probabilities of the text as local norm; our ability to perceive a statistical departure and restructure it as a norm is itself evidence of the essentially probabilistic nature of the language system. Our concern here, in any case, is not with psychological problems of the response to literature but with the linguistic options selected by the writer and their relation to the total meaning of the work. If in the selections he has made there is an unexpected pattern of frequency distributions, and this turns out to be motivated, it seems pointless to argue that such a phenomenon could not possibly be significant.

What cannot be expressed statistically is foregrounding: figures do not tell us whether a particular pattern has or has not 'value in the game'. For this we need to know the rules. A distinctive frequency distribution is in itself no guarantee of stylistic relevance, as can be seen from authorship studies, where the diagnostic features are often, from a literary standpoint, very trivial ones. Conversely, a linguistic feature that is stylistically very relevant may display a much less striking frequency pattern. But there is likely to be some quantitative turbulence, if a particular feature is felt to be prominent; and a few figures may be very suggestive. Counting, as Miller remarked, has many positive virtues; Ullmann offers a balanced view of this when he writes 'Yet even those who feel that detailed statistics are both unnecessary and unreliable [in a sphere where quality and context, aesthetic effects and suggestive overtones are of supreme importance] would probably agree that a rough indication of frequencies would often be helpful'.[11] A rough indication of frequencies is often just what is needed: enough to suggest why we should accept the writer's assertion that some feature is prominent in the text, and to allow us to check his statements. The figures, obviously, in no way constitute an analysis, interpretation or evaluation of the style.

But this is not, be it noted, a limitation on quantitative patterns as such; it is a limitation on the significance of prominence of any kind. Deviation is no more fundamental a phenomenon than statistical deflection: in fact there is no very clear line between the two, and in any given instance the most qualitatively deviant items may be among the least relevant. Thus if style cannot be reduced to counting, this is because it cannot be reduced to a simple question of prominence. An adequate characterization of an author's style is much more than an inventory of linguistic highlights. This is why linguists were so often reluctant to take up questions of criticism and evaluation, and tended to disclaim any contribution to the appraisal of what they were describing: they were very aware that statements about linguistic prominence by themselves offer no criterion of literary value. Nevertheless some values, or some aspects of value, must be expressed in linguistic terms. This is true for example of metrical patterns, which linguists have always considered their proper concern. The question is how far it is also true of patterns that are more directly related to meaning: what factors govern the relevance of 'effects' in grammar and vocabulary? The significance of rhythmic regularity has to be formulated linguistically, since it is a phonological phenomenon, although the ultimate value to which it relates is not 'given' by the language—that the sonnet is a highly valued pattern is not a linguistic fact, but the sonnet itself is. The sonnet form defines the

109

relevance of certain types of phonological pattern. There may likewise be some linguistic factor involved in determining whether a syntactic or a lexical pattern is stylistically relevant or not.

Certainly there is no magic in unexpectedness; and one line of approach has been to attempt to state conditions under which the unexpected is *not* relevant—namely when it is not really unexpected. Prominence, in this view, is not significant if the linguistically unpredicted configuration is predictable on other grounds; specifically, by reference to subject-matter, the implication being that it would have been predicted if we had known beforehand what the passage was about. So, for example, Ullmann warns of the danger in the search for statistically defined keywords: 'One must carefully avoid what have been called contextual words whose frequency is due to the subject-matter rather than to any deep-seated stylistic or psychological tendency'. Ullmann's concern here is with words that serve as indices of a particular author, and he goes on to discuss the significance of recurrent imagery for style and personality, citing as an example the prominence of insect vocabulary in the writings of Sartre;[12] in this context we can see that, by contrast, the prevalence of such words in a treatise on entomology would be irrelevant. But it is less easy to see how this can be generalized, even in the realm of vocabulary; is lexical foregrounding entirely dependent on imagery?

Can we in fact dismiss, as irrelevant, prominence that is due to subject-matter? Can we even claim to identify it? This was the third final question I asked earler, and it is one which relates very closely to an interpretation of the style of *The Inheritors*. In *The Inheritors*, the features that come to our attention are largely syntactic, and we are in the realm of syntactic imagery, where the syntax, in Ohmann's words, 'serves [a] vision of things': 'since there are innumerable kinds of deviance, we should expect that the ones elected by a poem or poet spring from particular semantic impulses, particular ways of looking at experience'.[13] Ohmann is concerned primarily with 'syntactic irregularities', but syntax need not be deviant in order to serve a vision of things; a foregrounded selection of everyday syntactic options may be just as visionary, and perhaps more effective. The vision provides the motivation for their prominence; it makes them relevant, however ordinary they may be. The style of *The Inheritors* rests very much on foregrounding of this kind.

The prominence, in other words, is often due to the vision. But

110

'vision' and 'subject-matter' are merely the different levels of meaning which we expect to find in a literary work; and each of these, the inner as well as the outer, and any as it were intermediate layers, finds expression in the syntax. In Ruqaiya Hasan's words, 'Each utterance has a thesis: what it is talking about uniquely and instantially; and in addition to this, each utterance has a function in the internal organization of the text: in combination with other utterances of the text it realizes the theme, structure and other aspects . . .'.[14] Patterns of syntactic prominence may reflect thesis or theme or 'other aspects' of the meaning of the work; every level is a potential source of motivation, a kind of semantic 'situational norm'. And since the role of syntax in language is to weave into a single fabric the different threads of meaning that derive from the variety of linguistic functions, one and the same syntactic feature is very likely to have at once both a deeper and a more immediate significance, like the participial structures in Milton as Chatman has interpreted them.[15]

Thus we cannot really discount 'prominence due to subject-matter', at least as far as syntactic prominence is concerned; especially where vision and subject-matter are themselves as closely interwoven as they are in *The Inheritors*. Rather, perhaps, we might think of the choice of subject-matter as being itself a stylistic choice, in the sense that the subject-matter may be more or less relevant to the underlying themes of the work. To the extent that the subject-matter is an integral element in the total meaning—in the artistic unity, if you will—to that extent, prominence that is felt to be partly or wholly 'due to' the subject-matter, far from being irrelevant to the style, will turn out to be very clearly foregrounded.

To cite a small example that I have used elsewhere, the prominence of finite verbs in simple past tense in the well-known 'return of Excalibur' lines in Tennyson's *Morte d'Arthur* relates immediately to the subject-matter: the passage is a direct narrative. But the choice of a story as subject-matter is itself related to the deeper pre-occupations of the work—with heroism and, beyond that, with the *res gestae*, with deeds as the realization of the true spirit of a people, and with history and historicalism; the narrative register is an appropriate form of expression, one that is congruent with the total meaning, and so the verb forms that are characteristically associated with it are motivated at every level. Similarly, it is not irrelevant to the *style* of an entomological monograph (although we may not be very interested in its style) that it

111

contains a lot of words for insects, if in fact it does. In stylistics we are concerned with language in relation to all the various levels of meaning that a work may have.

But while a given instance of syntactic or lexical prominence may be said to be 'motivated' either by the subject-matter or by some other level of the meaning, in the sense of deriving its relevance therefrom, it cannot really be said to be 'due to' it. Neither thesis nor theme imposes linguistic patterns. They may set up local expectancies, but these are by no means always fulfilled; there might actually be very few insect words in the work on entomology—and there are very few in Kafka.[16] There is always choice. In *The Inheritors*, Golding is offering a 'particular way of looking at experience', a vision of things which he ascribes to Neanderthal man; and he conveys this by syntactic prominence, by the frequency with which he selects certain key syntactic options. It is their frequency which establishes the clause types in question as prominent; but, as Ullmann has remarked, in stylistics we have *both* to count things *and* to look at them, one by one, and when we do this we find that the foregrounding effect is the product of two apparently opposed conditions of use. The foregrounded elements are certain clause types which display particular patterns of transitivity, as described in the next section; and in some instances the syntactic pattern is 'expected' in that it is the typical form of expression for the subject-matter—for the process, participants and circumstances that make up the thesis of the clause. Elsewhere, however, the same syntactic elements are found precisely where they would not be expected, there being other, more likely ways of 'saying the same thing'.

Here we might be inclined to talk of semantic choice and syntactic choice: what the author chooses to say, and how he chooses to say it. But this is a misleading distinction; not only because it is unrealistic in application (most distinctions in language leave indeterminate instances, although here there would be suspiciously many) but more because the combined effect is cumulative: the one does not weaken or cut across the other but reinforces it. We have to do here with an interaction, not of meaning and form, but of two levels of meaning, both of which find expression in form, and through the same syntactic features. The immediate thesis and the underlying theme come together in the syntax; the choice of subject-matter is motivated by the deeper meaning, and the transitivity patterns realize both. This is the explanation of their powerful impact.

112

The foregrounding of certain patterns in syntax as the expression of an underlying theme is what we understand by 'syntactic imagery', and we assume that its effect will be striking. But in *The Inheritors* these same syntactic patterns also figure prominently in their 'literal' sense, as the expression of subject-matter; and their prominence here is doubly relevant, since the literal use not only is motivated in itself but also provides a context for the metaphorical—we accept the syntactic vision of things more readily because we can see that it coincides with, and is an extension of, the reality. *The Inheritors* provides a remarkable illustration of how grammar can convey levels of meaning in literature; and this relates closely to the notion of linguistic functions which I discussed at the beginning. The foregrounded patterns, in this instance, are ideational ones, whose meaning resides in the representation of experience; as such they express not only the content of the narrative but also the abstract structure of the reality through which that content is interpreted. Sometimes the interpretation matches our own, and at other times, as in the drawing of the bow in passage A below, it conflicts with it; these are the 'opposed conditions of use' referred to earlier. Yet each tells a part of the story. Language, by the multiplicity of its functions, possesses a fugue-like quality in which a number of themes unfold simultaneously; each one of these themes is apprehended in various settings. Hence one recurrent motive in the text is likely to have more than one value in the whole.

*   *   *

The Inheritors[17] is prefaced by a quotation from H. G. Wells' *Outline of History*:

. . . We know very little of the appearance of the Neanderthal man, but this . . . seems to suggest an extreme hairiness, an ugliness, or a repulsive strangeness in his appearance over and above his low forehead, his beetle brows, his ape neck, and his inferior stature. . . . Says Sir Harry Johnston, in a survey of the rise of modern man in his *Views and Reviews*: 'The dim racial remembrance of such gorilla-like monsters, with cunning brains, shambling gait, hairy bodies, strong teeth, and possibly cannibalistic tendencies, may be the germ of the ogre in folklore. . . .'

The book is, in my opinion, a highly successful piece of imaginative prose writing; in the words of Kinkead-Weekes and Gregor, in their penetrating critical study, it is a 'reaching out through the imagination into the unknown'.[18] The persons of the story are a small band of Neanderthal people, initially eight strong, who refer to themselves as 'the people'; their world is then invaded by a group of more advanced stock, a fragment of a tribe, whom they call at first 'others' and later 'the new people'. This casual impact —casual, that is, from the tribe's point of view—proves to be the end of the people's world, and of the people themselves. At first and for more than nine-tenths of the book (pp. 1–216), we share the life of the people and their view of the world, and also their view of the tribe: for a long passage (pp. 137–80) the principal character, Lok, is hidden in a tree watching the tribe in their work, their ritual and their play, and the account of their doings is confined within the limits of Lok's understanding, requiring at times a considerable effort of 'interpretation'. At the very end (pp. 216–33) the standpoint shifts to that of the tribe, the in-heritors, and the world becomes recognizable as our own, or something very like it. I propose to examine an aspect of the linguistic resources as they are used first to characterize the people's world and then to effect the shift of world-view.

For this purpose I shall look closely at three passages taken from different parts of the book; these are reproduced below. Passage A is representative of the first, and much longer section, the narrative of the people; it is taken from the long account of Lok's vigil in the tree. Passage C is taken from the short final section, concerned with the tribe; while passage B spans the transition, the shift of standpoint occurring at the paragraph division within this passage. Linguistically, A and C differ in rather significant ways, while B is in certain respects transitional between them.

The clauses of passage A [56][19] are mainly clauses of action [21], location (including possession) [14] or mental process [16]; the remainder [5] are attributive.[20] Usually [46], the process is expressed by a finite verb in simple past tense. Almost all [19] of the action clauses describe simple movements (*turn, rise, hold, reach, throw, forward,* etc.); and of these the majority [15] are intransitive; the exceptions are *the man was holding the stick, as though someone had clapped a hand over her mouth, he threw himself forward* and *the echo of Liku's voice in his head sent him trembling at this perilous way of bushes towards the island.* The typical pattern is exemplified by the first two clauses, *the bushes twitched again* and *Lok steadied by the tree,* and there is no clear line, here, between action and location: both types have some reference in space, and both have one participant only. The clauses of movement usually [16] also specify location, e.g. *the man turned sideways in the bushes, he rushed to the edge of the water;* and
114

on the other hand, in addition to what is clearly movement, as in *a stick rose upright*, and what is clearly location, as in *there were hooks in the bone*, there is an intermediate type exemplified by [*the bushes*] *waded out*, where the verb is of the movement type but the subject is immobile.

The picture is one in which people act, but they do not act on things; they move, but they move only themselves, not other objects. Even such normally transitive verbs as *grab* occur intransitively: *he grabbed at the branches* is just another clause of movement (cf. *he smelled along the shaft of the twig*). Moreover a high proportion [exactly half] of the subjects are not people; they are either parts of the body [8] or inanimate objects [20], and of the human subjects half again [14] are found in clauses which are not clauses of action. Even among the four transitive action clauses, cited above, one has an inanimate subject and one is reflexive. There is a stress set up, a kind of syntactic counterpoint, between verbs of movement in their most active and dynamic form, that of finite verb in independent clause, in the simple past tense characteristic of the direct narrative of events in a time sequence, on the one hand, and on the other hand the preference for non-human subjects and the almost total absence of transitive clauses. It is particularly the lack of transitive clauses of action with human subjects (there are only two clauses in which a person acts on an external object) that creates an atmosphere of ineffectual activity: the scene is one of constant movement, but movement which is as much inanimate as human and in which only the mover is affected—nothing else changes. The syntactic tension expresses this combination of activity and helplessness.

No doubt this is a fair summary of the life of Neanderthal man. But Passage A is not a description of the people. The section from which it is taken is one in which Lok is observing and, to a certain extent, interacting with the tribe; they have captured one of the people, and it is for the most part their doings that are being described. And the tribe are not helpless. The transitivity patterns are not imposed by the subject-matter; they are the reflection of the underlying theme, or rather of one of the underlying themes—the inherent limitations of understanding, whether cultural or biological, of Lok and his people, and their consequent inability to survive when confronted with beings at a higher stage of development. In terms of the processes and events as we would interpret them, and encode them in our grammar, there is no immediate justification for the predominance of intransitives; this is the result of their being expressed through the medium of the semantic structures of Lok's universe. In our interpretation, a goal-directed process (or, as I shall suggest below, an externally caused process) took place: someone held up a bow and drew it. In Lok's interpretation, the process was undirected (or, again, self-caused): *a stick rose upright* and *began to grow shorter at both ends*. (I would differ slightly here from Kinkead-Weekes and Gregor, who suggest, I think, that the form of Lok's vision is perception and no more. There may be very little processing, but there surely is some; Lok has a theory—as he must have, because he has language.)

Thus it is the syntax as such, rather than the syntactic reflection of the subject-matter, to which we are responding. This would not emerge if we had no account of the activities of the tribe, since elsewhere—in the description of the people's own doings, or natural phenomena—the intransitiveness of the syntax would have been no more than a feature of the events themselves, and of the people's ineffectual manipulation of their environment. For this reason the vigil of Lok is a central element in the novel. We find, in its syntax, both levels of meaning side by side: Lok is now actor, now interpreter, and it is his potential in both these roles that is realized by the overall patterns of prominence that we have observed, the intransitives, the non-human subjects and the like. This is the dominant mode of expression. At the same time, in passage A, among the clauses that have human subjects, there are just two in which the subject is acting on something external to himself, and in both these the subject is a member of the tribe; it is not Lok. There is no instance in which Lok's own actions extend beyond himself; but there is a brief hint that such extension is conceivable. The syntactic foregrounding, of which this passage provides a typical example, thus has a complex significance: the predominance of intransitives reflects, first, the limitations of the people's own actions; second, the people's world view, which in general cannot transcend these limitations—but within which there may arise, thirdly, a dim apprehension of the superior powers of the 'others', represented by the rare intrusion of a transitive clause such as *the man was holding the stick out to him*. Here the syntax leads us into a third level of meaning, Golding's concern with the nature of humanity; the intellectual and spiritual developments that contribute to the present human condition, and the conflicts that arise within it, are realized in the form of conflicts between the stages of that development—and, syntactically, between the types of transitivity.

Passage A is both text and sample. It is not only these particular sentences and their meanings that determine our response, but the fact that they are part of a general syntactic and semantic scheme. That this passage is representative in its transitivity patterns can be seen from comparison with other extracts.[21] It also exemplifies certain other relevant features of the language of this part of the book. We have seen that there is a strong preference for processes having only one participant: in general there is only one nominal element in the structure of the clause, which is therefore the subject. But while there are very few complements,[22] there is an abundance of adjuncts [44]; and most of these [40] have some spatial reference. Specifically, they are (a) static [25], of which most [21] are place adjuncts consisting of preposition plus noun, the noun being either an inanimate object of the immediate natural environment (e.g. *bush*) or a part of the body, the remainder [4] being localizers (*at their farthest, at the end* etc.); and (b) dynamic [15], of which the majority [10] are of direction or non-terminal motion (*sideways, [rose] upright, at the branches, towards the island* etc.) and the remainder [5] perception, or at least circumstantial to some process that is not a physical one (e.g. *[looked at Lok] along his shoulder, [shouted] at the green drifts*). Thus with the dynamic type, either the movement is purely perceptual or, if physical, it never reaches a goal: the nearest thing to terminal motion is *he rushed to the edge of the water* (which is followed by *and came back!*).

The restriction to a single participant also applies to mental process clauses [16]. This category includes perception, cognition and reaction, as well as the rather distinct sub-category of verbalization; and such clauses in English typically contain a 'phenomenon', that which is seen, understood, liked, etc. Here however the phenomenon is often [8] either not expressed at all (e.g. *[Lok] gazed*) or expressed indirectly through a preposition, as in *he smelled along the shaft of the twig*; and sometimes [3] the subject is not a human being but a sense organ (*his nose examined this stuff and did not like it*). There is the same reluctance to envisage the 'whole man' (as distinct from part of his body) participating in a process in which other entities are involved.

There is very little modification of nouns [10, out of about 100]; and all modifiers are non-defining (e.g. *green drifts, glittering water*) except where [2] the modifier is the only semantically significant

117

element in the nominal, the head noun being a mere carrier demanded by the rules of English grammar (*white bone things*, *sticky brown stuff*). In terms of the immediate situation, things have defining attributes only if these attributes are their sole properties; at the more abstract level, in Lok's understanding the complex taxonomic ordering of natural phenomena that is implied by the use of defining modifiers is lacking, or is only rudimentary.

We can now formulate a description of a typical clause of what we may call 'Language A', the language in which the major part of the book is written and of which passage A is a sample, in terms of its process, participants and circumstances:

(1) There is one participant only, which is therefore subject; this is
   (a) actor in a non-directed action (action clauses are intransitive), or participant in a mental process (the one who perceives, etc.), or simply the bearer of some attribute or some spatial property;
   (b) a person (*Lok, the man, he*, etc.), or a part of the body, or an inanimate object of the immediate and tangible natural environment (*bush, water, twig*, etc.);
   (c) unmodified, other than by a determiner which is either an anaphoric demonstrative (*this, that*) or, with parts of the body, a personal possessive (*his*, etc.).

(2) The process is
   (a) action (which is always movement in space), or location-possession (including, e.g. *the man had white bone things above his eyes*, = 'above the man's eyes there were . . .'), or mental process (thinking and talking as well as seeing and feeling—a 'cunning brain'!—but often with a part of the body as subject);
   (b) active, non-modalized, finite, in simple past tense (one of a linear sequence of mutually independent processes).

(3) There are often other elements which are adjuncts, i.e. treated as circumstances attendant on the process, not as participants in it; these are
   (a) static expressions of place (in the form of prepositional phrases), or, if dynamic, expressions of direction (adverbs only) or of non-terminal motion, or of directionality of perception (e.g. *peered at the stick*);
   (b) often obligatory, occurring in clauses which are purely locational (e.g. *there were hooks in the bone*).

A grammar of Language A would tell us not merely what clauses occurred in the text but also what clauses could occur in that language. For example, as far as I know the clause *a branch curved downwards over the water* does not occur in the book; neither does *his hands felt along the base of the rock*. But both of them could have done. On the other hand, *he had very quickly broken off the lowest branches* breaks four rules: it has a human actor with a transitive verb, a tense other than simple past, a defining modifier and a non-spatial adjunct. This is not to say that it could not occur. Each of these features is improbable, and their combination is very improbable; but they are not impossible. They are improbable in that they occur with significantly lower frequency than in other varieties of English (such as, for example, the final section of *The Inheritors*).

Before leaving this passage, let us briefly reconsider the transitivity features in the light of a somewhat different analysis of transitivity in English. I have suggested elsewhere that the most generalized pattern of transitivity in modern English, extending beyond action clauses to clauses of all types, those of mental process and those expressing attributive and other relations, is one that is based not on the notions of actor and goal but on those of cause and effect.[23] In any clause, there is one central and obligatory participant—let us call it the 'affected' participant—which is inherently involved in the process. This corresponds to the actor in an intransitive clause of action, to the goal in a transitive clause of action and to the one who perceives, etc., in a clause of mental process; *Lok* has this function in all the following examples: *Lok turned away, Fa drew Lok away, Lok looked up at Fa, Lok was frightened, curiosity overcame Lok*. There may then be a second, optional participant, which is present only if the process is being regarded as brought about by some agency other than the participant affected by it: let us call this the 'agent'. This is the actor in a transitive clause of action and the initiator in the various types of causative; the function of *Tuami* in *Tuami waggled the paddle in the water* and *Tuami let the ivory drop from his hands*. As far as action clauses are concerned, an intransitive clause is one in which the roles of 'affected' and 'agent' are combined in the one participant; a transitive clause is one in which they are separated, the process being treated as one having an external cause.

In these terms, the entire transitivity structure of Language A can be summed up by saying that there is no cause and effect. More specifically: in this language, processes are seldom represented as resulting from an external cause; in those instances where they are, the 'agent' is seldom a human being; and where it is a human being, it is seldom one of the people. Whatever the type of process, there tends to be only one participant; any other entities are involved only indirectly, as circumstantial elements (syntactically, through the mediation of a preposition). It is as if doing was as passive as seeing, and things no more affected by actions than by perceptions: their role is as in clauses of mental process, where the object of perception is not in any sense 'acted on'—it is in fact the perceiver that is the 'affected' participant, not the thing perceived—and likewise tends to be expressed circumstantially (e.g. *Lok peered at the stick*). There is no effective relation between persons and objects: people do not bring about events in which anything other than they themselves, or parts of their bodies, are implicated.

There are, moreover, a great many, an excessive number, of these circumstantial elements; they are the objects in the natural environment, which as it were take the place of participants, and act as curbs and limitations on the process. People do not act on the things around them; they act within the limitations imposed by the things. The frustration of the struggle with the environment, of a life 'poised . . . between the future and the past' (Kinkead-Weekes and Gregor), is embodied in the syntax: many of the intransitive clauses have potentially transitive verbs in them, but instead of a direct object there is a prepositional phrase. The feeling of frustration is perhaps further reinforced by the constant reference to complex mental activities of cognition and verbalization. Although there are very few abstract nouns, there are very many clauses of speaking, knowing and understanding (e.g. *Lok understood that the man was holding the stick out to him*); and a recurrent theme, an obsession almost, is the difficulty of communicating memories and images (*I cannot see this picture*)—of transmitting experience through language, the vital step towards that social learning which would be a pre-condition of their further advance.

Such are some of the characteristics of Language A, the language which tells the story of the people. There is no such thing as a 'Language B'. Passage B is simply the point of transition between the two parts of the book. There is a 'Language C': this is the language of the last sixteen pages of the novel, and it is exemplified by the extract shown as passage C below. But passage B is of interest because it is linguistically also to some extent

120

transitional. There is no doubt that the first paragraph is basically in Language A and the second in Language C; moreover the switch is extremely sudden, being established in the first three words of B (ii), when Lok, with whom we have become closely identified, suddenly becomes *the red creature*. Nevertheless B (i) does provide some hints of the change to come.

There are a few instances (4) of a human 'agent' (actor in a transitive clause); not many, but one of them is Lok, in *Lok . . . picked up Tanakil*. Here is Lok acting on his environment, and the object 'affected' is a human being, and one of the tribe! There are some non-spatial adjuncts, such as *with an agonized squealing, like the legs of a giant*. There are abstract nominals: *demoniac activity, its weight of branches*. And there are perhaps more modifiers and complex verb forms than usual. None of these features is occurring for the first time; we have had forward-looking flashes throughout, e.g. (p. 191) *He had a picture of Liku looking up with soft and adoring eyes at Tanakil, guessed how Ha had gone with a kind of eager fearfulness to meet his sudden death;* and compare (pp. 212–13) '*Why did you not snatch the new one?*' and '*We will take Tanakil. Then they will give back the new one.*', both spoken by the more intelligent Fa (when transitive action clauses do occur in Language A, they are often in the dialogue). But there is a greater concentration of them in B (i), a linguistic complexity that is also in harmony with the increased complexity of the events, which has been being built up ever since the tribe first impinged on the people with the mysterious disappearance of Ha (p. 65). The syntax expresses the climax of the gradual overwhelming of Lok's understanding by new things and events; and this coincides with the climax in the events themselves as, with the remainder of the people all killed or captured, Lok's last companion, Fa, is carried over the edge of the waterfall. Lok is alone; there are no more people, and the last trace of his humanity, his membership of a society, has gone. In that moment he belongs to the past.

Lok does not speak again, because there is no one to speak to. But for a while we follow him, as the tribe might have followed him, although they did not—or rather we follow *it*; there can be no *him* where there is no *you* and *me*. The language is now Language C, and the story is that of *homo sapiens*; but for a few paragraphs, beginning at B (ii), as we remain with Lok, the syntax harks back to the world of the people, just as in B (i) it was beginning to look forward. The transition has taken place; *it was a strange creature, smallish, and bowed* that we had come to know so well. But it is still the final, darkening traces of this creature's world that we are seeing, fleetingly as if in an escaping dream.

A brief sketch of B (ii): There are very few transitive clauses of action [4]; in only one of these is Lok the agent—and here the 'affected' entity is a part of his own body: *it put up a hand*. The others have *the water* and *the river* as agent. Yet nearly half [22] the total number of clauses [47] have Lok as subject; here, apart from a few [4] mental process clauses, the verb is again one of simple movement or posture, and intransitive (*turn, move, crouch*, etc.; but including for the first time some with a connotation of attitude like *sidle* and *trot*; cf. *broke into a queer, loping run*). The remaining subjects are inanimate objects [19] and parts of the body [6]. But there are differences in these subjects. The horizons have widened; in addition to *water* and *river* we now have *sun* and *green sky*—a reminder that the new people walk upright: cf. (p. 143) *they did not look at the earth but straight ahead*; and there are now also human evidences and artefacts: *path, rollers, ropes*. And the parts of the body no longer see or feel; they are subjects only of intransitive verbs of movement (e.g. *its long arms swinging*), and mainly in non-finite clauses, expressing the dependent nature of the processes in which they participate. A majority [32] of the finite verbs are still in simple past tense; but there is more variation in the remainder, as well as more non-finite verbs [8], reflecting a slightly increased proportion of dependent clauses that is also a characteristic of Language C. And while in many clauses [21] we still find spatial adjuncts, these tend to be more varied and more complex (e.g. *down the rocks beyond the terrace from the melting ice in the mountains*).

This is the world of the tribe; but it is still inhabited, for a brief moment of time, by Lok. Once again the theme is enunciated by the syntax. Nature is no longer totally impenetrable; yet Lok remains powerless, master of nothing but his own body. In passages A and B taken together, there are more than fifty clauses in which the subject is Lok; but only one of these has Lok as an agent acting on something external to himself, one that has already been mentioned: *Lok picked up Tanakil*. There is a double irony here. Of all the positive actions on his environment that Lok might have taken, the one he does take is the utterly improbable one of capturing a girl of the tribe—improbable in the event, at the level of subject-matter (let us call this 'level one'), and improbable also in the deeper context ('level two'), since Lok's newly awakened power manifests itself as power over the one

122

element in the environment that is 'superior' to himself. It is at a still deeper 'level three' that the meaning becomes clear. The action gets him nowhere; but it is a syntactic hint that his people have played their part in the long trek towards the human condition.

By the time we reach passage C, the transition is complete. Here, for the first time, the majority of the clauses [48, out of 67] have a human subject; of these, more than half [25] are clauses of action, and most of these [19] are transitive. Leaving aside two in which the thing 'affected' is a part of the body, there is still a significant increase in the number of instances [17, contrasting with 5 in the whole of A and B together] in which a human agent is acting on an external object. The world of the inheritors is organized as ours is; or at least in a way that we can recognize. Among these are two clauses in which the subject is *they*, referring to the people ('the devils': e.g. *they have given me back a changeling*); in the tribe's scheme of things, the people are by no means powerless. There is a parallel here with the earlier part. In passage A the actions of the tribe are encoded in terms of the world view of the people, so that the predominance of intransitive clauses is interpreted at what we called 'level two', although there is a partial reflection of 'level one' in the fact that they are marginally less predominant when the subject-matter concerns the tribe. Similarly, in passage C references to the people are encoded in terms of the world view of the tribe, and transitive structures predominate; yet the only member of the people who is present—the only one to survive—is the captured baby, whose infant behaviour is described in largely intransitive terms (pp. 230–1). And the references to the people, in the dialogue, include such formulations as '*They cannot follow us, I tell you. They cannot pass over water*', which is a 'level one' reassurance that, in a 'level two' world of cause and effect whose causes are often unseen and unknown, there are at least limits to the devils' power.

We can now see the full complementarity between the two 'languages', but it is not easy to state. In Language A there is a level two theme, that of powerlessness. The momentary hints of potency that we are given at level one represent an antithetic variation which, however, has a significance at level three: the power is ascribed to the tribe but signifies Lok's own incipient awareness, the people's nascent understanding of the human potential. This has become a level two theme in Language C; and in like fashion the level two theme of Language A becomes in

Language C a level one variation, but again with a level three significance. The people may be powerless, but the tribe's demand for explanations of things, born of their own more advanced state, leads them, while still fearfully insisting on the people's weakness in action, to ascribe to them supernatural powers (Table 3).

While there are still inanimate subjects in the clause [11], as there always are in English, there is no single instance in passage C of an inanimate agent. In A and B we had *the echo of Liku's voice in his head sent him trembling . . .* , *the branches took her, the water had scooped a bowl out of the rock*; in C we have only *the sail glowed, the sun was sitting in it, the hills grow less*. Likewise all clauses with parts of the body as subject [8] are now intransitive, and none of them is a clause of mental process. Parts of the body no longer feel or perceive; they have attributes ascribed to them (e.g. *his teeth were wolf's teeth*) or they move (*the lips parted, the mouth was opening and shutting*). The limbs may move and posture, but only the whole man perceives and reacts to his environment. Now, he also shapes his environment: his actions have become more varied—no longer simply movements; we find here *save, obey* and *kiss*—and they produce results. Something, or someone, is affected by them.

Just as man's relation to his environment has altered, so his perception of it has changed; the environment has become enlarged. The objects in it are no longer the *twig, stick, bush, branch* of Language A, nor even the larger but still tangible *river, water, scars in the earth*. In passage B (ii) we already had *air* and *sun* and *sky* and *wind*; in C we have *the mountain . . . full of golden light, the sun was blazing, the sand was swirling* (the last metaphorically); and also human artefacts: *the sail, the mast*. Nature is not tamed: the features of the natural environment may no longer be agents in the transitivity patterns, but nor are they direct objects. What has happened is that the horizons have broadened. Where the people were bounded by tree and river and rock, the tribe are bounded by sky and sea and mountain. Although they are not yet conquered, the features that surround them no longer circumscribe all action and all contemplation. Whereas Lok *rushed to the edge of the water and came back*, the new people *steer in towards the shore*, and *look across the water at the green hills*.

*   *   *

The Inheritors has provided a perspective for a linguistic inquiry of a kind whose relevance and significance is notoriously difficult to assess: an inquiry into the language of a full-length prose work.

124

In this situation syntactic analysis is unlikely to offer anything in the way of new interpretations of particular sentences in terms of their subject-matter; the language as a whole is not deviant, and the difficulties of understanding are at the level of inter-pretation—or rather perhaps, in the present instance, re-inter-pretation, as when we insist on translating *the stick began to grow shorter at both ends* as 'the man drew the bow'. I have not, in this study, emphasized the use of linguistic analysis as a key; I doubt whether it has very much. What analysis can do is to establish certain regular patterns, on a comparative basis, in the form of differences which appear significant over a broad canvas. In *The Inheritors* these appear as differences within the text itself, between what we have called 'Language A' and 'Language C'. In terms of this novel, if either of these is to be regarded as a departure it will be Language C, which appears only briefly at the very end; but in the context of modern English as a whole it is Language A which constitutes the departure and Language C the norm. There is thus a double shift of standpoint in the move from global to local norm, but one which brings us back to more or less where we started.

The focus of attention has been on language in general, on the language system and its relation to the meanings of a literary work. In the study of the text, we have examined instances where particular syntactic options have been selected with a greater than expected frequency, that is partly but not wholly explained by reference to the subject-matter; and have suggested that, by considering how the meaning of these options, taken in the context of the ideational function of language as a whole, relates to an interpretation of the meaning of the work, one can show that they are relevant both as subject-matter and as underlying theme. Each sentence in the passages that were observed in detail is thus potentially of interest both in itself and as an instance of a general trend; and we have been able to ignore other differences, such as that between dialogue and narrative, although a study of these as sub-varieties would almost certainly yield further points of in-terest. Within the present context, the prominence that we have observed can be said to be 'motivated'; it is reasonable to talk of foregrounding, here, as an explanation of stylistic impact.

The establishment of a syntactic norm (for this is what it is) is thus a way of expressing one of the levels of meaning of the work: the fact that a particular pattern constitutes a norm *is* the meaning. The linguistic function of the pattern is therefore of some importance. The features that we have seen to be fore-grounded in *The Inheritors* derive from the ideational component in the language system; hence they represent, at the level at which they constitute a norm, a world view, a structuring of experience that is significant because there is no *a priori* reason why the experience should have been structured in this way rather than in another. More particularly, the foregrounded features were selections in transitivity. Transitivity is the set of options whereby the speaker encodes his experience of the processes of the external world, and of the internal world of his own conscious-ness, together with the participants in these processes and their attendant circumstances; and it embodies a very basic distinction of processes into two types, those that are regarded as due to an external cause, an agency other than the person or object in-volved, and those that are not. There are, in addition, many fur-ther categories and sub-types. Transitivity is really the corner-stone of the semantic organization of experience; and it is at one level what *The Inheritors* is about. The theme of the entire novel, in a sense, is transitivity: man's interpretation of his experience of the world, his understanding of its processes and of his own participation in them. This is the motivation for Golding's syn-tactic originality; it is because of this that the syntax is effective as a 'mode of meaning'.[24] The particular transitivity patterns that stand out in the text contribute to the artistic whole through the functional significance, in the language system, of the semantic options which they express.

This is what we understand by relevance: the notion that a linguistic feature 'belongs' in some way as part of the whole. The pursuit of prominence is not without significance for the under-standing and evaluation of a literary work; but nor is it sufficient to be a rewarding activity in itself. Dell Hymes said of phono-logical foregrounding that 'there must be appropriateness to the nexus of sound and meaning'; and this is no less true of the syntac-tic and semantic levels, where however the relationship is not one of sound and meaning but one of meaning and meaning. Here 'relevance' implies a congruence with our interpretation of what the work is about, and hence the criteria of belonging are semantic ones. We might be tempted to express the relevance of syntactic patterns, such as we find in *The Inheritors*, as a 'unity of form and meaning', parallel to the 'sound and meaning' formulation above; but this would I think be a false parallel. The syntactic categories are *per se* the realizations of semantic options, and the relevance is the relevance of one set of meanings to another—a relationship among the levels of meaning of the work itself.

In *The Inheritors*, the syntax is part of the story. As readers, we are reacting to the whole of the writer's creative use of 'meaning potential'; and the nature of language is such that he can convey, in a line of print, a complex of simultaneous themes, reflecting the variety of functions that language is required to serve. And because the elements of the language, the words and phrases and syntactic structures, tend to have multiple values, any one theme may have more than one interpretation: in expressing some content, for example, the writer may invite us at the same time to interpret it in quite a different functional context—as a cry of despair, perhaps. It is the same property of language that enables us to react to hints, to take offence and do all the other things that display the rhetoric of everyday verbal interaction. A theme that is strongly foregrounded is especially likely to be interpreted at more than one level. In *The Inheritors* it is the linguistic representation of experience, through the syntactic resources of transitivity, that is especially brought into relief, although there may be other themes not mentioned here that stand out in the same way. Every work achieves a unique balance among the types and components of meaning, and embodies the writer's individual exploration of the functional diversity of language.

Extracts from The Inheritors

A. (pp. 106–7.)
The bushes twitched again. Lok steadied by the tree and gazed. A head and a chest faced him, half-hidden. There were white bone things behind the leaves and hair. The man had white bone things above his eyes and under the mouth so that his face was longer than a face should be. The man turned sideways in the bushes and looked at Lok along his shoulder. A stick rose upright and there was a lump of bone in the middle. Lok peered at the stick and the lump of bone and the small eyes in the bone thing over the face. Suddenly Lok understood that the man was holding the stick out to him but neither he nor Lok could reach across the river. He would have laughed if it were not for the echo of the screaming in his head. The stick began to grow shorter at both ends. Then it shot out to full length again.

The dead tree by Lok's ear acquired a voice.

'Clop!'

His ears twitched and he turned to the tree. By his face there

127

had grown a twig: a twig that smelt of other, and of goose, and of the bitter berries that Lok's stomach told him he must not eat. This twig had a white bone at the end. There were hooks in the bone and sticky brown stuff hung in the crooks. His nose examined this stuff and did not like it. He smelled along the shaft of the twig. The leaves on the twig were red feathers and reminded him of goose. He was lost in a generalized astonishment and excitement. He shouted at the green drifts across the glittering water and heard Liku crying out in answer but could not catch the words. They were cut off suddenly as though someone had clapped a hand over her mouth. He rushed to the edge of the water and came back. On either side of the open bank the bushes grew thickly in the flood; they waded out until at their farthest some of the leaves were opening under water; and these bushes leaned over.

The echo of Liku's voice in his head sent him trembling at this perilous way of bushes towards the island. He dashed at them where normally they would have been rooted on dry land and his feet splashed. He threw himself forward and grabbed at the branches with hands and feet. He shouted:

'I am coming!'

B. (pp. 215–17.)
(i) Lok staggered to his feet, picked up Tanakil and ran after Fa along the terrace. There came a screaming from the figures by the hollow log and a loud bang from the jam. The tree began to move forward and the logs were lumbering about like the legs of a giant. The crumplefaced woman was struggling with Tuami on the rock by the hollow log; she burst free and came running towards Lok. There was movement everywhere, screaming, demonaic activity; the old man was coming across the tumbling logs. He threw something at Fa. Hunters were holding the hollow log against the terrace and the head of the tree with all its weight of branches and wet leaves was drawing along them. The fat woman was lying in the log, the crumpled woman was in it with Tanakil, the old man was tumbling into the back. The boughs crashed and drew along the rock with an agonized squealing. Fa was sitting by the water holding her head. The branches took her. She was moving with them out into the water and the hollow log was free of the rock and drawing away. The tree swung into the current with Fa sitting limply among the branches. Lok began to gibber again. He ran up and down on the terrace. The tree would not be cajoled or persuaded. It moved to the edge of the fall, it swung until it was lying along the lip. The water reared up over the trunk, pushing the roots were over. The tree hung for a while with the head facing upstream. Slowly the root end sank and the

128

head rose. Then it slid forward soundlessly and dropped over the fall.

(ii) The red creature stood on the edge of the terrace and did nothing. The hollow log was a dark spot on the water towards the place where the sun had gone down. The air in the gap was clear and blue and calm. There was no noise at all now except for the fall, for there was no wind and the green sky was clear. The red creature turned to the right and trotted slowly towards the far end of the terrace. Water was cascading down the rocks beyond the terrace from the melting ice in the mountains. The river was high and flat and drowned the edge of the terrace. There were long scars in the earth and rock where the branches of a tree had been dragged past by the water. The red creature came trotting back to a dark hollow in the side of the cliff where there was evidence of occupation. It looked at the other figure, dark now, that grinned down at it from the back of the hollow. Then it turned away and ran through the little passage that joined the terrace to the slope. It halted, peering down at the scars, the abandoned rollers and broken ropes. It turned again, sidled round a shoulder of rock and stood on an almost imperceptible path that ran along the sheer rocks. It began to sidle along the path, crouched, its long arms swinging, touching, almost as firm a support as the legs. It was peering down into the thunderous waters but there was nothing to be seen but the columns of glimmering haze where the water had scooped a bowl out of the rock. It moved faster, broke into a queer loping run that made the head bob up and down and the forearms alternate like the legs of a horse. It stopped at the end of the path and looked down at the long streamers of weed that were moving backwards and forwards under the water. It put up a hand and scratched under its chinless mouth.

C. (pp. 228–9.)
The sail glowed red-brown. Tuami glanced back at the gap through the mountain and saw that it was full of golden light and the sun was sitting in it. As if they were obeying some signal the people began to stir, to sit up and look across the water at the green hills. Twal bent over Tanakil and kissed her and murmured to her. Tanakil's lips parted. Her voice was harsh and came from far away in the night.
'Liku!'
Tuami heard Marlan whisper to him from by the mast.
'That is the devil's name. Only she may speak it.'
Now Vivani was really waking. They heard her huge, luxurious yawn and the bear skin was thrown off. She sat up, shook back her loose hair and looked first at Marlan then at Tuami. At once

he was filled again with lust and hate. If she had been what she was, if Marlan, if her man, if she had saved her baby in the storm on the salt water—

'My breasts are paining me.'

If she had not wanted the child as a plaything, if I had not saved the other as a joke—

He began to talk high and fast.

'There are plains beyond those hills, Marlan, for they grow less; and there will be herds for hunting. Let us steer in towards the shore. Have we water—but of course we have water! Did the women bring the food? Did you bring the food, Twal?'

Twal lifted her face towards him and it was twisted with grief and hate.

'What have I to do with food, master? You and he gave my child to the devils and they have given me back a changeling who does not see or speak.'

The sand was swirling in Tuami's brain. He thought in panic: they have given me back a changed Tuami; what shall I do? Only Marlan is the same—smaller, weaker but the same. He peered forward to find the changeless one as something he could hold on to. The sun was blazing on the red sail and Marlan was red. His arms and legs were contracted, his hair stood out and his beard, his teeth were wolf's teeth and his eyes like blind stones. The mouth was opening and shutting.

'They cannot follow us, I tell you. They cannot pass over water.'

(These extracts from William Golding's The Inheritors *are reprinted by permission of Faber & Faber Ltd.)*

This paper was first published in *Literary Style: a symposium,* ed. Seymour Chatman (O.U.P.).

NOTES

1. Bronislaw Malinowski, *Coral Gardens and their Magic,* Volume II. London: Allen & Unwin, 1935.
2. Nor the other way round, at least in the typical instances. There are certain linguistic activities in which one or other function is prescribed and the speaker required to supply the remainder: 'language exercises' such as 'Now ask your neighbour a question' (in foreign language classes), 'Write a sonnet' (in school).
3. Geoffrey N. Leech, ' "This bread I break"—language and interpretation'. *A Review of English Literature* 6.2, April 1965, 66–75 (p. 70).
4. René Wellek, 'Closing statement' (Retrospects and prospects from the viewpoint of literary criticism) in *Style in Language,* 408–19. (pp. 417–18).
5. Dell H. Hymes, 'Phonological aspects of style: some English sonnets', in *Style in Language,* 109–31. Reprinted in *Essays on the Language of Literature,* 33–53. (pp. 33–4).
6. On diatypic variation see Michael Gregory, 'Aspects of varieties differentiation'. *Journal of Linguistics* 3.2, 1967, 177–98.
7. Charles E. Osgood, 'Some effects of motivation on style of encoding', in *Style in Language,* 293–306 (p. 293).
8. Angus McIntosh, 'Saying'. *A Review of English Literature* 6.2, April 1965, 9–20. (p. 19). It is worth quoting further from the same paragraph: 'It is at least clear that any approach to this kind of problem which looks at anything less than the whole text as the ultimate unit has very little to contribute. Whatever it may be in linguistic analysis, the sentence is not the proper unit here. If there are any possibilities of progress, they must permeate long stretches of text and produce a gradual build-up of effect.'
9. Bernard Bloch, 'Linguistic structure and linguistic analysis', in A. A. Hill (ed.)., *Report of the Fourth Annual Round Table Meeting on Linguistics and Language Study.* Washington, D.C.: Georgetown University Press. Monograph Series on Languages and Linguistics, 1953, 40–4.
10. Josephine Miles, 'Eras in English poetry', in *Essays on the Language of Literature,* 175–96. (pp. 175–6).
11. See Stephen Ullmann, 'Style and personality'. *A Review of English Literature* 6.2, April 1965, 21–31. (p. 22).
12. Stephen Ullmann, op. cit., p. 29. See also his *Language and Style.* Oxford: Blackwell (Language and Style Series), 1964. (pp. 186–8).
13. Richard Ohmann, 'Literature as sentences', in *Essays on the Language of Literature,* 231–38. (p. 236). Originally published in *College English,* January 1966.
14. Ruqaiya Hasan, 'Linguistics and the study of literary texts'. *Études de Linguistique Appliquée* 5, 1967, 106–21 (pp. 109–10).

15. See Seymour Chatman, 'Milton's participial style'. *Publications of the Modern Language Association of America*, October 1968, 1386–1390.

16. *Metamorphosis* has, I believe, only two occurrences of an insect name, although 'crawl' is frequent.

17. William Golding, *The Inheritors*. London: Faber & Faber, 1955. 233 pp. Paperback edition, 1961. The pagination is the same in both.

18. Mark Kinkead-Weekes and Ian Gregor, *William Golding: a critical study*. London: Faber & Faber, 1967. 257 pp.

19. Figures in square brackets show numbers of occurrences. The most important of these are summarized in Table 2.

20. For a discussion of clause types see M. A. K. Halliday, 'Language structure and language function', in John Lyons (ed.), *New Horizons in Linguistics*. (Penguin).

21. The other extracts examined for comparison were three passages of similar length: p. 61 from *He remembered the old woman*; pp. 102–3 from *Then there was nothing more*; p. 166 from *At that the old man rushed forward*.

22. By 'complement' is understood all nominal elements other than the subject: direct object, indirect object, cognate object and adjectival and nominal complement. 'Adjuncts' are non-nominal elements (adverbs and prepositional phrases).

23. For discussions of transitivity see Charles J. Fillmore, 'The case for case', in Emmon Bach and Robert T. Harms (eds.), *Universals in Linguistic Theory*. New York: Holt, Rinehart & Winston, 1968, 1–88; M. A. K. Halliday, *Grammar, Society and the Noun*. London: H. K. Lewis (for University College London), 1967. pp. 32; M. A. K. Halliday, 'Notes on transitivity and theme in English' (Parts I and III), *Journal of Linguistics* 3.1, 1967, 37–81 and 4.2, 1968, 179–215.

24. See J. R. Firth, 'Modes of meaning'. *Essays and Studies (The English Association)*, 1951. Reprinted in J. R. Firth, *Papers in Linguistics 1934–1951*. London: Oxford University Press, 1957. 190–215.